What People Are Saying about Kris Murray
and Child Care Marketing Solutions

"We were struggling with enrollment and with separating ourselves from our competitors, which were mostly franchise and chain operations. There comes a point when you need someone who has in-depth knowledge about the specific industry you're in, and we've found that Kris is always fresh with the things she's learning and applying to our industry. Her ideas work—she has filled in the blanks for us. Kris really is the best we've been able to find to help us get fully enrolled and stay that way."

Tom and Mary Jo Runfola, Owners
Prep Academy Schools
Columbus, Ohio
www.prepacademyschools.org

"After ten years of operation and in the new economy, I was looking for something that could increase my enrollment and refresh my business. I found Kris Murray, and I absolutely love what her program has done for my business! She has taught me to look at my business in a whole different light. I have learned to use so many tools to help grow my business. In just three short months, I increased my enrollment by 49 percent! Amazing! Thank you, Kris, for helping me find that new passion and drive to make my child care the best it can be!"

Aleta Mechtel, Owner
Children of Tomorrow
Chanhassen, Minnesota
www.childrenoftomorrow.com

"Kris Murray has been extremely helpful in the marketing of my business. I have learned more in five weeks than I could have in any marketing class or training. My inquiries and tours have gone through the roof. I have enrolled eight families in five weeks, which is a huge success. I very much look forward to continuing this program and putting all that I've learned into play. Thank you so much for your help and support. I'm so thankful for you!"

Brynn Kelley, Owner
Scribbles and Giggles Child Care
Lansing, Michigan
www.scribblesandgiggleschildcare.com

"I had never needed to market my business until the economy crashed and I lost half of my enrollment. Until I met Kris, I knew nothing about marketing, and there was very little out there for child care center operators to glean from. Finding Kris and taking action have been paramount steps for rebuilding my business. In just three months, Kris gave me the tools to increase enrollment by 33 percent, and I will not stop there!"

Lynne Sutton, Owner
Kids Korner Children's Center
Williamsville, New York
www.kidskornerbuffalo.com

"Superb training! In my twenty-five-plus years in the business, I have only once had training of this caliber. Kris has taken marketing to the next level. I feel rejuvenated! I no longer feel like my marketing efforts are fruitless and a waste of money. My center's management team is more motivated than ever. We are Facebooking and e-mailing and video taping and, most important of all, *enrolling* new children! Hats off to Kris!"

Annette Gentry, Executive Director
Creative Day School
Greensboro, North Carolina
www.creativedayschool.net

"I've been in business for almost thirty-five years and have successfully run various large companies. For the past ten years, I've worked with my wife and partner, Jane Porterfield, who founded our child care centers twenty-five years ago. I can say that working with Kris has been unequivocally the single most successful contribution to my business life that I've experienced. There's not even a close second. I've long considered marketing one of my strongest assets. In retrospect, I suppose I did know a few things about marketing before working with Kris, but what I knew comprises maybe a quarter of what I know now—and I'm still learning new things from her. Unfortunately, it's not enough just to have high-quality staff, facilities, and programs for children. Kris has taught us how to effectively communicate this to our prospective families."

Gerry Pastor, Owner
Educational Playcare
Avon, Connecticut
www.educationalplaycare.com

The Ultimate Child Care Marketing Guide

THE ULTIMATE CHILD CARE MARKETING GUIDE

Tactics, Tools, and Strategies for Success

KRIS MURRAY

Redleaf Press®
www.redleafpress.org
800-423-8309

Published by Redleaf Press
10 Yorkton Court
St. Paul, MN 55117
www.redleafpress.org

First edition 2012
Cover design by Jim Handrigan
Cover photograph © iStockphoto.com/PeskyMonkey
Interior design by Mayfly Design
Typeset in Dante MT Std
Printed in the United States of America
18 17 16 15 14 13 12 11   1 2 3 4 5 6 7 8

Library of Congress Cataloging-in-Publication Data
Murray, Kris.
    The ultimate child care marketing guide : tactics, tools, and strategies for success / Kris Murray.
      p. cm.
    ISBN 978-1-60554-083-2 (alk. paper)
    1. Child care services—Management—Handbooks, manuals, etc. 2. Day care centers—Handbooks, manuals, etc. 3. Family day care—Handbooks, manuals, etc. 4. Marketing—Handbooks, manuals, etc. I. Title.
HQ778.5.M87 2012
362.71'20688—dc23
                                    2011036495
Printed on acid-free paper

*To the child care professionals who strive to provide a
high-quality, loving learning environment for our little ones.*

*For my mother, Barbara, who never stopped believing in me.
From you I inherited inner strength and determination.*

For my husband, Devin, who made this book possible. I love you.

Contents

Part 4: Media

Part 5: Tools for Success: Plans and Systems

Exercises and Figures

Exercises

Figures

Acknowledgments

I would like to thank Donna Kozik, my book-writing leader, who inspired me to write this book quickly and without hesitation. Thanks to my colleague and friend Julie Bartkus for being there and offering help and support. Thanks to my sister Wendy for constant love and support. You are my best friend. Thanks to Dan Kennedy and Bill Glazer for being my mentors in entrepreneurship and marketing that works. Thanks to my dear, departed dad for his entrepreneurial genius, some of which I hope to have inherited. Thanks to my children for the loving hugs and kisses and the pink orchid. I love you.

Introduction

I feel extremely fortunate to be a part of one of the worthiest and most important service sectors on our planet—the field of early childhood education and care. In my work as a child care business coach and marketing consultant, my mission and passion have been to help owners and directors in this field gain more control over their business. Through collaboration with these child care leaders, I've been able to contribute to the growth and stability of high-quality early learning programs. For me, nothing is more fulfilling than having a positive impact on young children.

Over the past few years, I've worked with hundreds of early childhood business owners and directors around the globe. In some cases, I helped them successfully build their child care programs from scratch. In other cases, when they were struggling mightily during the economic collapse and on the verge of shutting their doors, I helped them survive.

Based on what has worked for these child care leaders, as well as on twenty-two years of studying small business marketing, I bring you here the best ideas and strategies for growing your early childhood program in any economic circumstance. For some of you, that's going to mean learning how to increase your enrollment to fill your program to capacity—and then to manage a waiting list to keep it full. For others, including those with already fully enrolled programs, that's going to mean improving your business skills, systems, and return on investment to ensure you make the most of your marketing dollars. Regardless, you'll be glad you picked up this book!

In my experience, I've found that only 15 to 20 percent of child care leaders have had any formal training in business-related topics such as marketing, sales, or accounting. Indeed, early childhood professionals are much more likely to think of themselves as educators than business leaders. Therefore, the chances are pretty good you're one of the 80 to 85 percent of early childhood business owners or directors who could benefit from training in how to market and grow your child care program. Take comfort—*The Ultimate Child Care Marketing Guide* will start you on your journey to becoming a more business-savvy leader, even an entrepreneurial thinker. And that's a good thing.

The exercises and action steps in this guide are specifically designed to help early childhood leaders accomplish the following goals:

- Create tracking and measurement systems so you can easily discover what strategies are working and what strategies are not.
- Gain insight into which marketing strategies are bringing you the most inquiries and enrollments.
- Understand what groups of people comprise your market and how to learn more about them.
- Leverage the goodwill of your happy clients by getting powerful testimonials and referrals.
- Identify how your program is unique from others in your area and communicate that uniqueness effectively.
- Use your marketing message to set your program apart and get noticed by your prospects.
- Determine what's preventing you from converting more prospective families into enrolled families.
- Use highly targeted media to reach your best prospects.
- Understand more about the ever-changing world of online media and how to use it to promote your program.
- Understand the basic elements of a marketing plan and how to put one into action.

What Is Marketing?

What's your definition of *marketing*? While some people define marketing as advertising or enrollment building, I find these definitions too narrow. I define marketing as getting and keeping customers. That's what marketing is all about, pure and simple.

Broadly put, your marketing needs to

- make qualified prospects aware of your program;
- aid in the selling of your services to those qualified prospects;
- convert those prospects into your customers; and
- help keep your customers enrolled for as long as possible.

So does that mean that crafting a high-quality child care program is marketing? Yes, if it helps you get and retain customers—which it most certainly does! What about working with your staff to improve their communication skills with parents? Absolutely! That's marketing too. By reading this book and doing the exercises in it, you will be well on your way to taking concrete steps toward improving the effectiveness of your marketing activities and filling your child care program to capacity.

The Ultimate Child Care Marketing Guide is based on marketing concepts that have consistently produced results for early childhood owners and directors just like you. In fact, I can't wait to share with you the real-world success strategies that dozens of my clients use. These clients range from a woman in Albuquerque, New Mexico, just starting her home-based family child care program, to a husband-wife team who own four large child care centers near Hartford, Connecticut. Whether you're trying to expand your church preschool from ten to twenty children, or you have multiple large locations, you will be able to use the ideas in this book to market your program more effectively and be at capacity over the long run.

The methodology I teach is based on what I call the *four pillars of marketing*, which are shown in the following illustration.

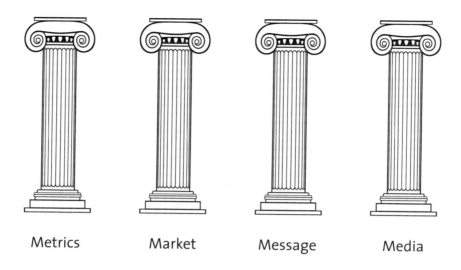

| Metrics | Market | Message | Media |

The four pillars provide another way for you to think about marketing, or getting the right message to the right market using the right media, and measuring your ongoing success with metrics. Going a bit deeper now, I define the four pillars of marketing like this:

1. *Metrics* are how you track and measure the performance of your marketing activities.
2. *Market* is the groups of people in your area that are important to your program—customers, prospects, competitors, staff members, and community business partners—and the trends that impact them.
3. *Message* is the words, images, and ideas in your marketing materials and efforts.
4. *Media* are the methods you use to promote your program, such as advertising, e-mail, the Internet, and printed brochures.

The four pillars of marketing provide a solid framework for learning the business concepts in this book. However, some marketing-related ideas important to your program do not fit into a specific pillar. For example, how does the concept of sales fit into marketing? And what about "enrollment building"? Sales and enrollment building are both marketing processes that are vital to your program's success. Once you get the right message to your market using the right media, your sales process kicks in. It's what you do to build your enrollment, once prospects discover you exist. Your marketing plan is the framework for all these processes to work together.

The information in *The Ultimate Child Care Marketing Guide* will provide you with all the skills, knowledge, and tools you need to market to and find your best customers—ones who are the *best fit* for your program's offerings—and keep them with you until the children outgrow your program.

Now Take Action!

You, as the owner or director of your program, need to be the responsible and accountable party to ensure that your marketing is optimized and that your enrollment-building processes are in place. Don't expect anyone else to fully understand what it takes to get your program enrolled to capacity and keep it that way over the long term. *You* must be the marketing champion of your early childhood enterprise! Leaders who delegate this all-important responsibility make the mistake of thinking someone else will care enough to make sure your best prospective customers discover and contact your program, take a tour, and enroll. Please don't make this mistake.

The Ultimate Child Care Marketing Guide is divided into four parts, one for each marketing pillar. Following each part, you'll find a section called *Now Take Action!* containing a series of questions to help you implement what you've learned right away. I strongly believe implementation is the key to success. You aren't going to see many results when you just think, study, and talk to your peers and staff—you simply must take action to see results. Implement the action steps with as much speed as you can muster, and don't implement just one at a time. Employ as many action steps as you can, all at once, a technique sometimes referred to as *taking massive action*. The biggest benefits of taking massive action are fast results and a huge boost in momentum. The progress you make when you take massive action will inspire you to keep taking more and more.

Are you ready to get started? Great! As my dad always used to say to my brother and me when we were little, "Let's roll!"

Metrics

You must do the things you think you cannot do.
—Eleanor Roosevelt

Bite off more than you can chew, then chew it.
—Ella Williams

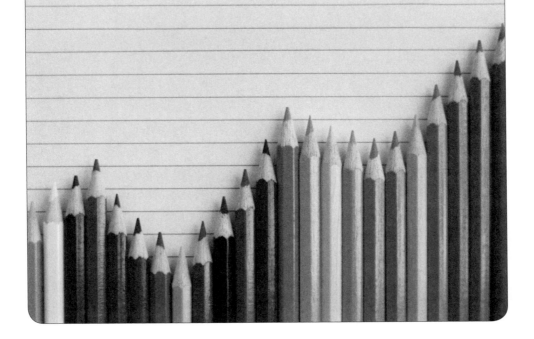

1

Keeping Score

Many child care business owners and directors make business decisions based on gut instinct, an adventuresome spirit, or desperation. But it's the owners and directors that make decisions based on data whose programs grow quickly and steadily over time.

The most reliable method for making positive changes in your child care program is to do just that—make decisions based on specific marketing data. It's critical that you keep score of, or track, your child care program's marketing and financial performance over time. This is where metrics enter the picture. *Metrics* can be defined as the numbers and data you track in your business numbers that indicate how your business is performing. Metrics are what you use to keep score. Not tracking data, or not tracking the right data, is one of the most common reasons why small businesses—child care programs included—stay small or cease to exist.

 Meet Tom and Juanita from Illinois. Tom and Juanita have owned ABC Learning Center for nearly sixteen years. ABC Learning Center is an accredited, high-quality child care program with a licensed capacity of 128 children. Until the recession of 2008, Tom and Juanita's program was fairly full, ranging from 85 to 95 percent of capacity. Then, like many child care businesses in the United States, their enrollment decreased dramatically in fall 2008 because parents were losing their jobs. Enrollment declined from 118 children at its peak in 2008 to just 63 children by January 2009.

Tom and Juanita were scared, frustrated, and living week to week, trying to make payroll. They couldn't figure out how to market their business effectively, because they had never really needed to—they had always relied successfully on word of mouth. Tom and Juanita had a friend with some experience in marketing local businesses, so they hired him to help update their website and implement some radio and newspaper advertising. They spent $3,000 on marketing but got just a handful of inquiries and only one new enrollment during the entire three-month period. To make matters worse, they had no systems in place to track the progress of their enrollment-building efforts over time. They knew they had to take fast and decisive action to save their business.

Tom went bowling with his buddies and shared his concerns and frustrations. Tom's friend Mark recommended that he try some tracking tools Mark had created for his own chiropractic business—he called them metrics. When he got home that night, Tom excitedly told Juanita they were going to get serious about tracking the important metrics in their child care business, starting the very next day.

We'll learn more about Tom and Juanita's journey throughout this book. With metrics, you're going to be able to eliminate the guesswork and take action based on real data. Let's get started.

Four Categories of Metrics

Marketing metrics fall into four categories:

- customer value and acquisition metrics
- enrollment funnel metrics
- marketing return on investment metrics
- retention rate metrics

Here's more about each category.

Customer Value and Acquisition Metrics

Customer value and acquisition metrics illustrate the relationship between the revenue a typical customer family brings to your program compared to the average amount of money you spend to market to and acquire that family as a customer. Customer value and acquisition metrics produce numbers with tremendous power, because they provide great clarity and insight into a fundamental business relationship: the financial value of a typical customer to your program in contrast to how much your business spends to acquire that customer.

Three of the nine metrics covered in part 1 of this book are included in the customer value and acquisition category:

- lifetime customer value
- cost per lead
- cost per new customer

Enrollment Funnel Metrics

An *enrollment funnel* is simply the process you undertake to market and promote your center to generate leads. *Leads* (also referred to as prospects or inquiries) are prospective customers who contact you for more information, take a tour of your facility, and eventually enroll in your program. *Enrollment funnel metrics* measure the results of each step in your marketing process in order to determine each step's effectiveness in converting leads to enrollments.

There are three metrics to measure in this category:

- raw number of leads
- conversion ratio of leads to tours
- conversion ratio of tours to enrollments

Marketing Return on Investment (ROI) Metrics

Marketing return on investment metrics provide you with information about every action you take to advertise, promote, or market your program. When you use marketing return on investment, or ROI, metrics, you know which messages or media choices are performing the best for you—that is, bringing you new prospects and enrollments—and which are not. This, too, is a tremendously powerful measurement, because it tells you where you're getting the best bang for your marketing buck. Then, the next time you have to do an enrollment-building campaign, you can implement only the best performing promotions.

Of the nine metrics covered in this part of the book, one metric falls into the marketing return on investment category:

- return on investment by marketing expenditure

Retention Rate Metrics

Retention rate metrics provide you with a picture of how well and how long you hold on to two key resources in your program: customers and staff. There are two metrics in this category:

- customer retention rates
- staff retention rates

These two individual metrics often go hand in hand. For example, if your program has a relatively high level of staff turnover, especially compared to your competition, it's almost a sure bet you're struggling to keep customers in your program. Parents and young children do not do well with a high level of teacher turnover. Teacher turnover can often be the number one reason families leave a center or school.

Get Savvy

Savvy business owners control their own marketing campaigns, and they hold themselves and their staff accountable for the consistent tracking of important marketing information. Setting up and tracking the nine core marketing metrics requires time and effort, to be sure, but I know of no other single thing that will bring you a bigger payoff. I guarantee that tracking these nine metrics in your child care business is the best thing you can do to get a handle on effective marketing, to grow your enrollment, and to dramatically improve the financial health of your program—probably in just a few months. How do I know? Because my clients tell me over and over that the number one thing that helped them increase their enrollment was tracking their metrics using the exact methods I share with you in this book.

The chapters that follow tackle each one of the nine metrics. They tell you how to get your metrics tracking systems set up, and they provide you with the tools you need to start using them. Once you get the tracking systems in place and use them consistently, you'll be amazed by the concrete, data-driven information at your fingertips! And you'll find that the systems can be simple and easy to maintain—and very enlightening. The numbers generated by the metrics you track will tell you precisely what's happening in your child care business, as well as where you need to focus your attention next. Imagine the relief you'll feel when you can base your business decisions on real data rather than on gut instinct. You'll wonder how you ever got along before!

2

Customer Value and Acquisition Metrics

Customer value and acquisition metrics illustrate the relationship between the revenue a typical customer brings to your program compared to the average amount of money it takes to market to and acquire that customer. There's tremendous power in these numbers, because they can provide you with insights and clarity about how you're doing at getting and keeping new clients.

Lifetime Customer Value

So what is *lifetime customer value* or LCV? Simply put, it's the monetary value a typical customer brings to your business, in *gross revenue* and in *net revenue*, over the course of time that they do business with you. Lifetime customer value (sometimes referred to as total customer value) is one of the core metrics that all small business owners should track over time. Unfortunately, very few early childhood leaders I've met do so on a consistent basis, if at all.

Knowing the monetary value a typical family brings to your business is an important tool, because it provides a guideline for how much money you can afford to invest in marketing to attract and then enroll a family in your program. Once you know your lifetime customer value, you will feel more in control and confident as a business owner or director.

I recommend that you track this metric by *family* in the program rather than by *child* in the program, because when one child is enrolled in a program, 99 percent of the time Mom or Dad will enroll all of their children there. And your marketing campaign will speak to the family as a whole, not to a single child within a family. (In some cases, however, you will want to track metrics based on each child, such as your room-by-room enrollment compared to capacity.)

Let's dig in a bit deeper. If you know that your average LCV is $20,000 in enrollment revenue, then you can feel confident about investing $300 in your marketing campaign to gain a new customer. Because at the end of the day, spending $300 on marketing costs to obtain a new customer who will bring $20,000 in tuition revenue to your program is a darn good return on your investment! Not to mention $20,000 in gross sales revenue! If your marketing can perform at that level consistently, your program would likely be highly profitable. Further, if you have a for-profit business, it can also be useful to calculate your LCV on a net profit basis. You would do this the same way as in the earlier example, but rather than using top-line enrollment revenue, you would use the net profit amount from your financial statement for that same period. (If you need help setting up a financial statement—also known as a profit-and-loss statement—consult your bookkeeper or accountant.)

To calculate your LCV, you need to be able to determine the average length of enrollment by family. Determining the average length of enrollment by family can be a bit tricky—especially if your enrollment records are incomplete. If you're not doing so already, start keeping accurate records of when each family and child begins and ends your program. You can use a software program like Microsoft Excel to do this fairly easily, or run reports from whatever child care management software system you're using.

Another easy method for determining the average length of enrollment by family is to compile a written list of all the families enrolled with you during a given period, and then highlight the families who are no longer with your program. For just those departed families, add up the number of months each of them was your customer, from the date their first child enrolled in the program through the date their youngest child graduated from or left the program. Then add up the months of enrollment for all of the departed families combined, and divide that total by the number of departed families being considered.

1. Number of families who graduated out of or otherwise left program during a given time frame   = _____
2. Combined number of months each family identified in line 1 was enrolled   = _____
3. Average length of enrollment equals line 2 divided by line 1   = _____

Doing this will give you your average length of enrollment.

Now that you know your average length of enrollment, you can calculate your LCV. Here are the steps you'll take. An exercise follows on the next page.

1. Determine the total annual gross revenue (also referred to as sales or tuition) that your child care center generated over the last twelve months, according to your financial statement.
2. Determine the number of typical families you had enrolled during that period.
3. Determine the average annual revenue per family by dividing the revenue (step 1) by the number of families (step 2). Determine the average length of enrollment.
4. Divide the number of months (step 4) by 12 to get an average yearly length of enrollment.
5. Multiply the number of years (step 5) by the average annual revenue per family (step 3).

Let's take a look at each of the steps through the experience of Tom and Juanita.

 Juanita and Tom, the owners of ABC Learning Center, followed the advice of their friend Mark. They started by calculating the lifetime customer value of their child care center. They were curious about the monetary impact of one typical family on their program, so they calculated their LCV by looking over their enrollment records from the last couple of years. Here is what they found.

1. Determine the total annual gross revenue generated over the last twelve months, according to financial statement: In Tom and Juanita's case, the total annual gross revenue for 2010 was $610,000.

2. Determine the number of typical families enrolled during that period: Tom and Juanita took the total number of families they had on the books for each month during 2010 and divided it by twelve, which came out to an average of 61 families.

3. Determine the average annual revenue per family by dividing the revenue (step 1) by the number of families (step 2): Tom divided $610,000 by 61 families for an average annual value of $10,000 per family. $10,000 is the value that the typical family brought to Tom and Juanita's program during the entire year of 2010.

4. Determine the average length of enrollment: Tom and Juanita looked at all the families who left or graduated in 2010 and found that there were 25 families. These 25 families were customers of ABC Learning Center for a total of 750 months, or an average of 30 months (750 months divided by 25 families).

5. Divide the number of months (step 4) by 12 to get an average yearly length of enrollment: Tom and Juanita divided 30 months by 12, to get an average length of 2.5 years.

6. Multiply the number of years (step 5) by the average annual value per family (step 3): Tom and Juanita calculated $10,000 per family in step 3, so they multiplied it by an average length of enrollment of 2.5 years. Their current lifetime customer value is $25,000 ($10,000 x 2.5).

Are you ready to track the LCV of *your* program? It's pretty simple, really. Just follow the steps in the exercise below.

Exercise 1 Determine Your Program's Lifetime Customer Value

Complete this exercise at least once per year and track results over time.

1. Total annual gross revenue last 12 months = $_____

2. Total number of enrolled families (not enrolled children) = _____

3. Average annual revenue per family (line 1 divided by line 2) = $_____

4. Average length of enrollment (combined number of months
   divided by line 2)   = $_____

5. Average length of enrollment (years) (line 4 divided by 12) =   _____

6. Lifetime customer value (multiply line 3 by line 5)   = $_____

Do this exercise to calculate your program's LCV on a regular basis. I recommend you do so at least once a year, and if possible every six months. Give yourself a six-month window to accurately collect the data you need. So at the end of 2012, look at your financial statement and enrollment records from July 1, 2010, through June 30, 2011. Then on June 30, 2012, do the exercise again for the next period, January 1, 2011, through December 31, 2011, and so on.

In general, child care centers have a very high LCV compared to other types of consumer service businesses, such as restaurants, carpet cleaners, orthodontists, and even family attorneys. Most of the child care programs I work with have an LCV ranging from $18,000 to $50,000. (Remember, the LCV equals the tuition revenue that one typical family brings to your program over the entire time they are enrolled with you.) In comparison, a midpriced restaurant may have an LCV of around $3,000 based on an average customer who spends $50 per dining experience and frequents the restaurant once a month for five years ($50 x 12 x 5 = $3,000). The point is, most child care programs have the advantage of having a higher lifetime customer value, which means they can count on more revenue per customer than other service businesses. If your LCV is five times higher than the midpriced restaurant down the street, you may be able to invest up to five times more in your marketing campaigns while still being extremely profitable. This is especially true if you have a high rate of average customer retention—three, four, or even five years for example—which will be true for you if the majority of your client families stay enrolled in your program from the time their children are infants through to kindergarten and beyond.

As I said earlier, knowing the monetary value a typical family brings to your child care business, by calculating your LCV and tracking it over time, is a powerful tool. I hope you feel excited about and empowered by it. Knowing your LCV provides ultimate clarity regarding what you can afford to invest in your marketing campaigns.

Cost Per Lead

The next metric to measure is your *cost per lead* (also referred to as cost per inquiry). Just as a lead is a prospective parent who shows interest in your program, your cost per lead is the amount of money you spend, on average, to get one new customer inquiry—a phone call from a parent looking for child care, for instance, after seeing an ad you ran in the neighborhood newspaper. Knowing your cost per lead is important because it helps you track how effectively your marketing is performing in terms of bringing new prospects to your program.

The cost per lead metric is also a great tool for planning your marketing budget. For example, if you convert 10 percent of inquiries to enrollments, and you know how much you spent to acquire each lead, then you can roughly calculate how many marketing dollars you will need to spend to get a targeted number of new enrollments.

Follow the steps in the exercise below to calculate your cost per lead metric. Do this exercise on a quarterly basis, a week or two after the end of each quarter. For instance, for first quarter (January through March), you would calculate the metric around the middle of April.

Exercise 2 Calculate Your Cost Per Lead

Complete this exercise on a quarterly basis and track results over time.

1. Total marketing expenditures over the prior 3 months (including all advertising, promotion, events, signage, and website updates, among others)   = $_____

2. Total prospective customers (leads) that contacted your center by any method (such as walk-ins, telephone, or web) during that same period   = _____

3. Cost per lead (divide line 1 by line 2)   = $_____

As with all of the metrics in this book, I recommend measuring your cost per lead over time on a consistent basis. If you notice you're spending a lot more marketing dollars to get the same number of leads from quarter to quarter, then you can take action by finding more inexpensive methods—online marketing, press releases, or printed flyers—of lead generation. (We will discuss the relative costs of different methods of marketing and lead generation in much more detail in later chapters.)

Take into account not only the quantity of leads, but also the quality. Your marketing should bring in leads that are a *market match* for you—that is, prospective customers who are a good fit for your program. For example, if your program is priced at the higher end of the market, then your ideal customers will likely live in an affluent neighborhood in your area. To ensure the best chance of converting leads to enrollments, you'll want to generate as many leads as possible from the segments of the market that are the best match. Focus your marketing efforts on specific *market segments*, or niches, in your area that are a good match for your program, and you'll bring in more leads overall, a higher rate of which will be likely to convert to enrollments.

Cost Per New Customer

Now that you're tracking your cost per lead metric, it makes sense to calculate your *cost per new customer* (or cost per sale) too—that is, the amount of money you spend, on average, to convert one customer lead to one new customer. In fact, the cost per new customer metric is an even more important metric to track than cost per lead. The reason? If your marketing is driving in a ton of new leads, but, for example, your staff is lousy at converting those leads to enrollments, you'll end up wasting a lot of marketing money. Track your enrollment process to make sure prospective customers become enrolled customers.

The following exercise will help you calculate the cost per new customer metric.

Exercise 3 Calculate Your Cost Per New Customer

Complete this exercise on a quarterly basis and track results over time.

1. Total marketing expenditures over the prior 3 months   = $_____

2. New enrollments during that same period   = _____

3. Cost per new customer (divide line 1 by line 2)   = $_____

The goal of tracking these two metrics—cost per lead and cost per new customer—over time is to get smarter about which marketing messages help you build enrollment. As you get more sophisticated and savvy about what messages work best, your costs per lead and per new customer will decrease—which means your marketing efforts are becoming more effective and cost-efficient.

Create a monthly or quarterly graph from your cost per lead and cost per new customer results; see figure 2-1. In fact, do this for all of your metrics over time. You'll be better able to understand how your business is doing and have an easy tool to use when sharing results with your team.

Figure 2-1: Average Cost Per Lead and Average Cost Per New Customer

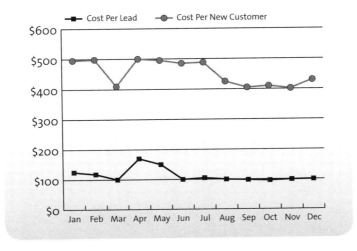

Tom and Juanita calculated their cost per lead and their cost per new customer and discovered they were spending only $20 per lead during an average month. They were getting very few inquiries, but they were also spending very few marketing dollars. Their cost per new customer was $100, as shown below.

Figure 2-2: Cost Per Lead and Cost Per New Customer at ABC Learning Center

Amount spent on marketing over the prior 3 months:	$800.00
Number of leads during that period:	40
Cost per lead:	$20.00
Number of new enrollments during that period:	8
Cost per new customer:	$100.00

Tom and Juanita realized that compared to their program's LCV of $25,000, they could afford to spend more to get more quality inquiries and leads. Remember, they needed to grow their program by sixty-five more children to be at capacity. They'll need to do a lot more marketing to fill their program quickly. But how will they make sure their marketing works for them this time around?

Through the exercises and examples in this chapter, I hope you understand more about the importance of customer value and acquisition metrics, and how they fit together. Earlier in the book, I gave my personal definition of *marketing*: getting and keeping customers. The metrics in this chapter provide you with the knowledge of exactly how much money you're spending to get customers and how much revenue they are providing your program in return. Knowing this is essential to becoming a skilled and savvy marketer.

3

Enrollment Funnel Metrics

When you think of an enrollment funnel, what comes to mind? Some marketing experts use the term "marketing funnel" to describe the process by which leads are converted into customers, and that's where *enrollment funnel* comes from. I created the idea of an *enrollment funnel metric* to help child care leaders visualize their programs' enrollment-building processes: Leads enter the enrollment funnel when parents contact care providers to gather information to make a child care purchasing decision, and they exit the funnel when families have been converted into customers—or not. During the time that prospective customers are in the funnel, program leaders have the opportunity to communicate with them, build rapport with them, and give them reasons to take action—that is to say, to enroll their children in your program.

An enrollment funnel has three key phases:

1. inquiry by a prospective parent
2. conversion of that inquiry into a tour of your facility and program
3. conversion of that tour into an enrollment

Accordingly, the next three metrics in this part of the book allow you to quantify each of the three phases of the enrollment funnel:

- raw number of leads (or inquiries)
- conversion ratio of leads to tours
- conversion ratio of tours to enrollments

Raw Number of Leads (or Inquiries)

The first metric in the enrollment funnel category is the *raw number of leads* (or inquiries), which is simply the total number of prospective families who inquire about your child care program during a given period. There are several good reasons to track this metric:

You will become aware of the peaks and valleys of enrollment activity during the calendar year. When you are aware of your business's enrollment cycles throughout the year, you can prepare for them by timing your marketing efforts—and budget—appropriately. If, for example, you always have a high volume of leads in August, as many child care centers do, you and your staff can be better prepared for the increased number of phone call inquiries, e-mail inquiries, and, ideally, tours. On the flip side, you may want to plan your marketing expenditures for the times of the year that are traditionally more quiet.

You will become aware of increases and decreases in lead volumes over time. Information about year-over-year trends in your business is extremely valuable for understanding the dynamics of your market's economy as well as supply and demand. When you are aware of your business's year-over-year enrollment trends (comparing data from January 2010 to data from January 2009, for example), you will be better able to plan appropriately for staff needs, scheduling, and resources and supplies.

You will know how many leads are in your enrollment funnel, which allows you to forecast enrollments. When you know how many leads are in your enrollment funnel, you will be able to fairly accurately forecast the number of new enrollments you should receive based on your current performance of converting inquiries into enrollments, a process known as *conversion ratio*. Conversion ratio will be discussed in depth later in this chapter.

I recommend setting up a simple system to keep track of the raw number of leads metric by month. You can do this on a spreadsheet, or by hand, by keeping the data compiled in a notebook or binder so you have it together in one resource. Then you can create a visual graph or chart of monthly and yearly trends, which might look something like this:

Figure 3-1: Raw Number of Leads Per Month

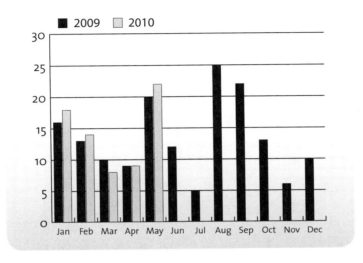

By tracking monthly leads over a long period of time, you will have a deeper understanding of what to expect for your program in terms of new prospects, as well as for when you should expect your phone to ring the most. Knowing these things is the first step to understanding what's happening in your enrollment funnel.

Collecting Information about Prospective Customers

In addition to tracking and counting your raw number of leads, you need a reliable system for collecting key information about each prospect who contacts you. This information is extremely valuable, because it allows you to follow up effectively with your prospects over time, and the process of gathering the information is an opportunity to build rapport and trust with the parent who is seeking child care. One of the biggest mistakes you can make is to work hard getting your phone to ring with new prospects, but then not have a system in place to ensure you and your staff are collecting as much information as possible about each prospect. If you're relying on a system of scraps of paper and sticky notes to gather prospect information, then you're leaving money on the table! Use the following form—or create your own—to collect and preserve the important information.

Figure 3-2: Prospect Inquiry Form

Today's Date: _____

Staff Member's Name: _____ Time of Day: _____

Prospect's Name: _____

# of Children: _____

Children's Names: _____ Date of Birth: _____

_____ Date of Birth: _____

_____ Date of Birth: _____

Address: _____ City / State: _____

Zip: _____ Phone Number(s): _____

E-mail Address: _____

Tour Date: _____ How Prospect Heard about Us: _____

_____

Notes: _____

_____

Regardless of what type of tool you use to record the information about each prospective customer, make sure you have a tracking system in place for doing so. And make sure everyone on your staff is trained to use the tracking system—step by step, each time they speak with a prospective customer, with no exceptions: it's important to capture information about each prospect in a consistent, systematic way, no matter who answers the phone at your center. Again, the worst thing for your program is to leave this information tracking process up to chance. You and your staff must have the discipline to make sure everyone is recording each lead effectively.

Generate More Leads

As I said at the start of this chapter, the primary goal of your ongoing marketing efforts should be the generation of leads—getting the phone to ring with new prospects. This is the important first step for getting and keeping your enrollment at capacity and building a waiting list. Don't worry—I'll provide you with many ideas for how to generate more leads later in this book.

 Before Tom and Juanita began systematically tracking their raw number of leads and consistently gathering information about each prospect, they had no idea how many leads they were generating every month. So they pulled out all their files for the previous year and started compiling some reasonably accurate data based on the lists of inquiries and tours they did have. Over the previous year, they realized, ABC Learning Center had received an average of only ten new inquiries per month. Tom and Juanita knew they needed to drive up the raw number of leads to have any hope of substantial growth in enrollment, and now that they were tracking their prospects, they could set a definitive goal: to double the number of leads within two months. They began forming a plan to bring in at least twenty inquiries per month within sixty days.

Conversion Ratio of Leads to Tours

The next metric in the enrollment funnel category is the *conversion ratio of leads to tours*. Now that you're tracking the raw number of leads coming in, and systematically collecting key information about each prospect, you're ready to begin tracking the rate at which people who inquire about your child care program actually visit your facility and take a tour.

The first step in calculating this metric is to create an easy tool for you and your staff to use to record, along with other basic information, whether or not a prospective customer actually comes in for a tour. The prospect status form that follows is an example of a straightforward way to keep tabs on the status of prospective customers. Use it—or create your own.

Figure 3-3: Prospect Status Form

Contact Date	Prospect Name	Phone Number	Source of Lead	Toured?	Date Toured	Enrolled?	Date Enrolled	Follow-Up Status
Feb 15	Mary Smith	333-555-1212	Referral from the Johnsons	Yes	Feb. 16	No		Sent thank-you note, then called
Feb 19	Peter Jones	333-555-6789	Website	Not yet				Sent thank-you note, then called

You should track your leads by date and record each prospect's name and phone number; this information can be transferred directly from your prospect inquiry form (shown on page 26). Also record information regarding the way the prospect heard about your business, and whether—and when—they take a tour. Reserve space on the form to track the status of your follow-up with each lead or to remind yourself and your staff that follow-up needs to be initiated. Add a new row to your prospect status form for each family that inquires. You'll easily be able to count up all the leads you've received and tours you've given during a particular time frame.

Follow-up

Let's take a moment to discuss follow-up. One of the biggest mistakes I've seen child care leaders make is not following up with prospects. As you know, many parents are not ready to make immediate decisions about child care, and sometimes it takes several months for them to commit to a program. After all, they generally hope to stay enrolled in one program for several years of their young child's life, so it's a huge decision. Therefore, you *must* have in place a follow-up process that includes, ideally, several types of contact methods; don't follow up just by calling parents on the telephone.

Based on actual results of experiences my clients have had with different methods of follow-up, the most effective follow-up involves sending communications—thank-you notes, greeting cards, letters, and postcards—to parents' home mailing address. E-mail is a fantastic tool for follow-up, too, because it's inexpensive and easy to automate. (See chapter 16 for information on keeping your e-mail and website up to date.)

The point is, if you are only calling your prospect on the phone once or twice after the tour, which is what many child care leaders do, it's very likely you will dramatically improve your leads-to-tours conversion ratio by adding some direct mail and e-mail follow-up to your process. (Again, we'll discuss follow-up strategies and sequences in more detail later on.)

Calculate Your Leads-to-Tours Conversion

Once you have your prospect status and follow-up system in place, it will be easy for you to look back and track your leads-to-tours conversion ratio at the end of every month. You may, however, decide to do this analysis every quarter rather than every month, because it can often take people several weeks or months to make a decision about which child care to choose. Quarterly tracking is fine. They key is to be sure to track consistently over the long term.

Here's how to calculate your leads-to-tours conversion ratio. Simply divide the number of tours given by the number of inquiries received in a given period. For example, if you gave four tours in March and received ten inquiries, you would divide four by ten and get a ratio of 0.4, or 40 percent.

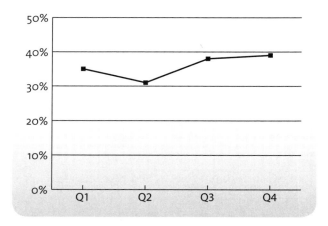

Figure 3-4: Conversion Ratio of Leads to Tours by Quarter

Most programs that do a good job with their telephone and e-mail customer inquiry processes can expect at least a 20 to 40 percent conversion ratio of leads to tours. Put another way, for every ten inquiries, two to four of them will convert into program tours. If your conversion ratio of leads to tours is lower than 20 percent, you'll want to figure out why people are choosing not to take your tour. For example, is there something about the way you or your staff handle phone inquiries that's turning prospects off? Perhaps the person answering your phone needs some training to better develop her telephone sales skills. Perhaps she needs a cheat sheet on what to say when a prospective customer calls or some customer service role-play and practice. Or maybe she just needs tips on how to communicate the program's benefits and features in a friendly and professional manner.

Improve Your Leads-to-Tours Ratio

Once you've calculated your leads-to-tours conversion ratio, you're ready to develop a plan for improving it. The first step in your improvement plan is to set a clear goal for what you want to accomplish and then communicate it to your staff. For example, if you currently convert 40 percent of leads to tours, you might set a goal to hit a 50 percent conversion rate in the next month. Then you will want to test some new strategies for achieving that goal and track your progress. Again, make sure to include your staff in all the aspects of this plan.

What are some concrete strategies you can use to convert more inquiries to tours? Many of my child care clients use the following ideas and see fantastic results almost immediately. The best way to start is to take a few simple but highly focused actions, test your results, tweak the strategies to work for your program, and keep implementing over time. Here are a few of the simplest but most effective ideas:

Make a great first impression on the telephone. You and your staff have about seven seconds to make a great first impression with your prospect on the phone. So, if you are answering the phone in the middle of a stressful situation, you may need to check yourself and your phone demeanor, put the prospect on hold until you collect yourself, or even delegate the call to a staff member who is not harried. If you take a deep breath and smile, you can convey a happier, more relaxed attitude to the caller on the other end.

Build trust and rapport with your prospects. I cannot think of a purchase decision that is more deeply based on trust and rapport than a mother making a child care decision. This is one reason why parent testimonials, reviews, and success stories are so vital to your marketing toolbox. They do a better job of building trust with your prospect than you can. When you are on the phone with a prospect, you can build rapport immediately by asking her to tell you a little bit about her child, such as the child's personality or interests. Parents, especially moms, love to talk about their children. So before you do any selling of your program, you can build great rapport by spending five or ten minutes chatting about the child.

Another great rapport builder is to ask the prospect why she is seeking care. Did she recently move to the area or have a job change, or is she newly pregnant? Or perhaps her current child care situation is less than optimal. Knowing the landscape of why she is calling you will make it that much easier to present your program to her in a way that matches what she is looking for.

Identify your prospect's needs, wants, fears, and concerns. After you build trust and rapport, you want to identify your customer's needs. The outcome of this is to find a problem, want, or need the prospect has that your product or service can solve. The easiest way to find such information is to ask questions. Make a list of key questions you can ask the prospect to identify his need, fears, desires, and concerns. One great question you can ask is, "What is *most* important to you about choosing child care for your child?" or "What are your biggest concerns about selecting the right child care program?"

Analyze the process you use to speak with prospects when they call your program for the first time. Are you communicating clearly what's unique about your program? The goal of each phone inquiry is to bring the prospect in for a tour of your program. Role-play the phone inquiry process with your staff and make sure they are trained on how to best communicate what's different about your program, build rapport with the prospective customer, and ask for the tour.

Create incentives that will motivate people to visit your program. Incentives can range from a free children's event for the community, a free gift raffle (such as a children's book, a small gift basket, or a T-shirt), or a presentation by an interesting guest speaker. Give families a reason to get to know you and visit your program. Add a level of fun and creativity by tying the free gift to an upcoming holiday or season. For example, you could create a special event around Dr. Seuss's birthday and offer free Dr. Seuss books. You might even schedule a guest appearance by the Cat in the Hat!

Conversion Ratio of Tours to Enrollments

Once you've begun tracking your ratio of leads to tours, you can go on to the next step in your enrollment funnel—tracking the *conversion ratio of tours to enrollments*, which is the third and last metric in the enrollment funnel category. This metric will tell you what portion of the people who tour your program end up enrolling in your program.

Once you've given the tour, record that you've done so on the prospect status form. You'll also want to review your tour notes, record any pertinent details about the tour, and plan your follow-up with the prospective customer. Record on the prospect status form whether the prospective customer enrolls and the enrollment date. Recording this information will easily allow you to count the number of new enrollments you've received during a given time frame.

Now you're ready to calculate your conversion ratio of tours to enrollments. Here's how. Simply divide the number of enrollments by the number of tours for that period. For example, if you had three enrollments in the second quarter and ten tours, you would divide three by ten and get a ratio of 0.3, or 30 percent. When you put your monthly or quarterly ratio metrics on a graph, you can get a great visual indication of what's taking place in your enrollment funnel over time. Is it improving or declining? Is it up and down? Figure 3-5 illustrates an example of this shown by quarter.

Figure 3-5: Conversion Ratio of Tours to Enrollments by Quarter

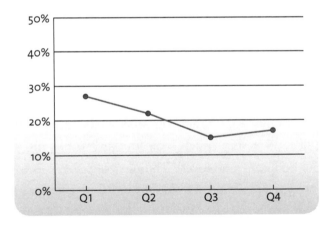

As with the leads-to-tours ratio, once you've calculated your tours-to-enrollments conversion ratio, you're ready to develop a plan for improving it. Again, the first step in your improvement plan is to set a clear goal for what you want to accomplish, and communicate it to your staff. For example, if you currently convert 30 percent of tours to enrollments, you might set a goal to hit a 35 percent conversion rate in the next month.

Ideas for Converting More Tours to Enrollments

To improve your conversion ratio of tours to enrollments, you've got to make some changes to how you and your staff conduct the tour. Here are some ideas to try:

Make a tour checklist. Use a tour checklist to make sure your child care program stands out. Test your checklist by asking a friend (not a member of your staff) to take the tour as a "mystery shopper." Take notes on the quality and effectiveness of the tour as you go, and improve the checklist accordingly. Remember, you want to make a good first impression to every prospective customer. When you make an awesome first impression, your enrollment will increase.

See appendix A for a tour checklist you can use to make sure your program is putting its best face forward during tours.

Ask for the enrollment. You don't have to give your prospect the hard sell, but you do have to make sure you and your staff are *asking* the prospect for their business. One way to ease into this is to ask the prospect, "What's most important to you about choosing child care?" If the prospect says, "Security and safety," then you can highlight your program's safety features. Next you might say something like, "We very much look forward to helping your son learn, grow, thrive, and be happy and loved. The next step for us is to simply fill out this enrollment form, and we'll get his cubby and folder set up." You could even start helping the prospect fill out the form, acting confidently that your program is the best choice Mom or Dad could make. If you hesitate or are afraid to ask for their enrollment, your prospect will likely respond with, "I need to talk to my husband"; "I just started looking"; or "I need to think about it."

Handle objections elegantly. There is an art to handling objections and closing the sale, especially in a child care setting. The best way to handle objections is to make a list of all the possible objections your prospects could give, and then creatively come up with a way to address and conquer each one. Practice responding to objections ahead of time so that you feel comfortable when they come up with the prospect.

Tie performance to staff compensation. You can tie staff compensation to all three steps in the enrollment funnel by offering a substantial bonus program. Make sure your staff knows the goals you've established for each step by presenting the metrics of your current funnel to your staff and explaining your ideas for achieving each goal. Properly train your staff to communicate effectively on the phone with prospective customers, as well as how to conduct prospect tours using new strategies. Last, train staff to feel comfortable asking for the enrollment at the end of a tour, and motivate them by providing incentives.

> **TIP:** I teach a five-week "virtual" course that focuses on using scripts and role-play techniques to learn how to elegantly ask for the enrollment and handle objections. For more information, visit www .enrollmentbootcamp.com.

Improve the curb appeal of your facility. When was the last time you objectively viewed your facility from the outside? Have you driven by your competitors' facilities and really studied their *curb appeal*—the attractiveness of their facilities and grounds from the outside—and compared it to your own? Is the way your facility looks on the outside sending the wrong message to your prospects? You can make improvements by planting neat-looking shrubs and flowers, mulching beds, cleaning up debris, removing peeling paint, updating your signage, and replacing any worn or sagging fixtures.

Pay attention to details. It's often the little things that moms and dads notice during a tour. For example, consider stashing away a supply of breath mints for the staff; make sure teachers are not gossiping, texting, or talking on cell phones; have and enforce a professional dress code, making sure staff tattoos are covered; and make sure the facility smells good.

I hope you can see now that making just a few small improvements to this critical piece of your marketing puzzle can have a huge impact on your program's enrollment. Many of my clients and students tell me that getting this part of their tracking system in place is the most important thing they learned from my trainings, because it had the biggest impact on their success.

 Now that they were systematically tracking their leads, Tom and Juanita were able to learn that about 60 percent of their leads were coming from online searches (primarily via Google) and about 20 percent were coming from their referral-rewards program. The remaining 20 percent were from other sources, such as direct mail, community events, and general word of mouth.

Because the majority of their leads were coming from online searches, they decided to implement an online advertising and promotional campaign to drive more online traffic to their program. To meet their goal of bringing in at least twenty leads per month within sixty days, Tom and Juanita launched an online marketing campaign, which included banner ads, a new virtual tour video and video testimonials on their website, a series of YouTube videos, and a new Facebook fan page—in addition to a targeted direct mail campaign, print ads, and press releases. Within just thirty days of implementing this campaign, they started to see their phone and e-mail inquiries increase substantially. They used their new tracking systems to continually measure their progress and tweak the marketing plan over time.

Figure 3-6: Tom and Juanita's Enrollment Funnel: Actual versus Goal

Average Activity Per Month	Actual—Previous 3 Months	Goal—Next 2 Months
Leads	10	20
Conversion ratio:	40%	50%
Tours	4	10
Conversion ratio:	25%	35%
New enrollments	1	4

Figure 3-7: Conversion Rates by Quarter for ABC Learning Center

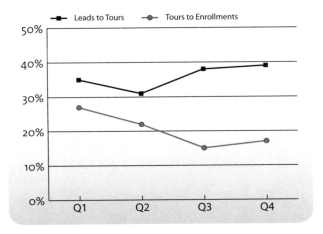

Figure 3-7 illustrates the conversion rates that Tom and Juanita were getting for ABC Learning Center. They tracked their results quarterly and found that while their conversion rate of leads to tours was improving over time, their conversion rate of tours to enrollments was declining. There was evidently a problem with the way they were conducting their tours—or perhaps something else was amiss. Tom and Juanita knew they quickly needed to determine what the problem was and how to fix it. They knew they needed more concrete data, so they decided to send an e-mail follow-up questionnaire to all the prospective parents who toured over the last three months but did not enroll. They also hired a consultant to act as a mystery shopper of their program as well as their competitors, to make sure their tour was on par with other programs in their market.

They discovered that their pricing was a bit out of whack compared to their competitors—they were charging a much higher initial enrollment and registration fee than the other programs in town, so they reduced the enrollment fee to make it more affordable for parents to get started. They also got feedback that parents were concerned about their lack of a secure entrance with cameras, so they added a locked door with keypad and exterior cameras at the entrance. They looked forward to tracking their tour-to-enrollment conversion ratio to see if these improvements would provide results. They also took the very smart step of communicating in a follow-up letter to all their prospects the changes they had made.

Consistent tracking of your enrollment funnel over time is one of the most important things a child care owner or manager can do to grow her program and get the biggest return on her marketing budget. Remember, whatever you measure, you can manage. Use your enrollment funnel metrics to gain clarity on exactly what to do to improve your enrollment-building and marketing processes.

4

Marketing Return on Investment Metrics

When you keep score of how your marketing efforts are performing, the most important thing to measure is your return on investment—that is, what you spend to market your services compared to how much revenue that marketing produces for your business. When set up properly, *marketing return on investment (ROI) metrics* provide you with information about every marketing action you take to advertise, promote, or sell your program. When you use marketing return on investment metrics, you'll know which marketing messages or methods perform best for you in terms of bringing you new prospects and enrollments. This is powerful information, because when you know what marketing efforts bring you the best bang for your marketing buck, you can focus on doing only the best performing marketing the next time you need to do an enrollment-building campaign.

Return on Investment by Marketing Expenditure

Have you ever heard the saying, "I know half my marketing is working; I just don't know which half!" When you track the marketing ROI of your advertising and promotional efforts, you will discover how much revenue each effort generates compared to its cost. As a result, you will have a much better idea of exactly which marketing activities are working effectively and which ones are bringing you zero prospects or enrollments. Knowing your ROI by marketing expenditure will help you feel in control of your marketing budget and confident about how your marketing dollars are being spent.

Unique Identifiers

The key to knowing your ROI by marketing expenditure is to create a system that attaches a unique code or phrase—an identifier—to each marketing activity you do. A *unique identifier* allows you to track the number of leads a specific marketing activity generates.

For example, let's say you want to test a direct mail campaign to families in your area using postcard mailers. If you include a unique identifier—such as an offer code, a unique phone number, or a unique website address—you'll be able to use the identifier to track the number of prospects and enrollments the postcard campaign brings you. You can then measure the estimated long-term revenue you'll receive from those enrollments and measure the projected return on investment of that specific marketing activity.

So the first step to start measuring your marketing ROI is to make sure each marketing activity has a unique identifier—something that will allow you to track it. There are several unique identifiers you can use:

Unique offers and unique offer codes. To use a unique offer or a unique offer code to identify a marketing activity, begin by coming up with one or more special offers to include on a particular direct mailer or ad campaign. To claim the offer, the prospective customer would have to reference the unique offer, such as "Save $300 on Enrollment," or provide you with the unique offer code printed on the mailer or ad, such as "Use offer code Summer300." When a customer provides you with the unique offer or the unique offer code, you would document which marketing effort the offer or code was attached to and which generated the new lead.

Using different special offers for different segments of your mailing list helps you test which special offers bring you the most leads. For example, if you were to divide your direct mail list into thirds, you could send one-third of the recipients a mailer that offers them 50 percent off one month's tuition when they use offer code "50off"; one-third might receive an offer that saves them $300 on tuition when they use offer code "300Special"; and one-third might get a $200 gift card upon enrollment when they use offer code "Gift-Card200." When the customer provides you with the code, you would record it in whatever tracking tool you have set up for that purpose—in this book, we've shown it being tracked on the prospect status form on page 28.

Unique phone numbers. Did you know there are telephone tracking companies that can easily and affordably supply unique phone numbers that you can exclusively tie to a specific marketing effort or campaign? The telephone tracking company assigns a specific call tracking number to each marketing initiative and then integrates it into the corresponding advertisement, website page, e-mail newsletter, direct mail campaign, or any other marketing activity. A unique phone number enables you to automatically track the number of inquiries coming in because of a specific marketing effort or campaign.

A unique phone number is a highly effective method of tracking your marketing ROI, because it offers the most accurate record. It does not rely on human memory—an employee remembering to ask each prospect how she heard about your program, or the prospect accurately recalling what promotion motivated her to pick up the phone, for instance. The data for each unique phone number is compiled by the tracking company, which supplies you with a performance report about each of the phone numbers. The report can include the volume of calls that came in for each number and the average length of the phone calls, among other data. Based on which inbound line prospects called, you will be able to see which marketing efforts produced the highest volume of calls and track which prospects book a tour and then enroll.

 Tom and Juanita were so excited about the insights they received when they implemented their enrollment funnel metrics that they asked their friend Mark to help them track the performance and return on investment of their marketing activities. Mark referred them to the company he uses for his chiropractic practice—a company that specializes in using unique and trackable telephone number data to measure the performance of Mark's different print ads, online banner ads, flyers, and direct mailers. Tom and Juanita got set up with ten unique local phone numbers, all programmed to ring inbound to the center's main phone line. This service cost ABC Learning Center about $150 per month.

Hiring a phone tracking company is fairly affordable—I've been told that plans start at about $100 per month. Pricing for this type of tracking service is primarily based on your expected call volume (or the estimated click volume for your website; more on unique websites below). If you're spending $5,000 or more annually on your marketing, this approach may make sense for you, because it will essentially pay for itself—you will *save* money over the long run when you're able to eliminate the marketing activities that do not produce results.

Another benefit of setting up and tracking unique phone numbers is that the inbound calls are recorded, which allows you to monitor the way your employees are answering the phone and engaging with prospects. The recordings can become part of your customer service audit, and you can set up goals for your staff based on what you hear. As a result, these unique phone numbers can become a training tool for helping your staff improve the way they communicate with prospects and convert phone inquiries to tours.

> **TIP:** Several companies provide these phone tracking metrics—some local and some nationwide. Two that you might want to research are CallFire (www.callfire.com) and Mongoose Metrics (www.mongoosemetrics.com).

Unique website addresses. For your online marketing efforts, you can set up unique web page addresses and measure the volume of traffic coming from those pages. For example, you might test the idea of sending prospects to a special web page to get your free offer, such as a free parenting DVD or a child care checklist. You can test which offer performs better by comparing the web page traffic reports—that is, by looking at how many unique visitors came to those offer pages. Your website manager or hosting company should be able to provide you with a statistics report for all the pages of the websites you own.

Customer feedback. If you don't want to set up unique phone numbers or website addresses or use special offer codes, you can always resort to the good old-fashioned method of determining your marketing effectiveness by asking each prospective customer, "How did you hear about us?" The customer feedback method is less reliable and accurate than the other methods because it requires your prospect to accurately recall what motivated him to call you, and because it relies on you and your staff to consistently ask for and write down the customer's response. In some cases, your prospective customer won't have a code or remember how she heard about you—and that's okay. And because you're promoting your center all the time and in a variety of ways, it's likely you'll have customers come to you because of more than just one promotion, or through word of mouth. Even so, if you and your staff consistently ask each prospect how he heard of you, you'll be able to estimate the ROI of each marketing effort and how effective it is over time. It's perfectly okay if your ROI figures are estimates based on the data you do have. ROI is not an exact science; you only need your numbers to be reasonably reliable.

Calculating ROI

Now that we've discussed the unique identification methods you can use, let's learn more about the steps for actually calculating your marketing ROI. Let's use the example of a magazine advertisement that runs in one issue of a monthly publication.

After the ad has run, you can tally all the inquiries you received about that ad and how many of those leads resulted in new enrollments for your program. Again, it may take a few months for the data to be completely accurate, because it can take that long for some prospects to make their child care decision. So if this ad ran in the August issue of a magazine, you might wait until November to determine how many enrollments were generated from it. Let's say you determine that you received one new enrolling family from this ad, and they have two young children. The next step is to estimate the annual revenue you will receive from this family. If the ad cost $300 to run and you receive $12,000 in tuition revenue over the next twelve months from this family, the annual return on investment for this ad would be 40:1. That is, for every dollar you spent, you earned $40. This is an excellent return on investment, and you would want to continue advertising in this magazine.

Now assume you put each of your marketing activities in a chart or table and measure them against one another to see which one performs the best. The following figure illustrates this approach for the time of August through November of a given year.

Figure 4-1: Return on Investment by Marketing Effort/Campaign: August through November

Marketing Effort	Cost	# of Inquiries	# of Families Enrolled	Cost Per Inquiry	Cost Per New Customer	Annual Revenue Generated	ROI
Magazine ad	$300	3	1	$100	$300	$12,000	40x
Program website	$100	10	3	$10	$33	$26,000	260x
Online coupon site	$74	2	—	$37	—	—	—
Postcard mailer	$500	10	5	$50	$100	$50,000	100x
TOTAL	$974	25	9	$39	$108	$88,000	90x

You can see from this table that the best performing marketing activity is the program's website, which generated ten inquiries and three new enrolling families, for an ROI of 260 to 1. The second best performer is the postcard mailer, which had an ROI of 100 to 1. The online coupon site, which produced no new enrollments, is the poorest performing activity. Therefore, this program should discontinue the online coupon site promotion or else make substantial changes to the ad copy, images, or offer before testing it again.

 By tying unique phone numbers or offer codes to each marketing activity, Tom and Juanita were able to compile their marketing return on investment metrics for ABC Learning Center. As shown in the following table, the highest ROI activities were the referral program and the website/online ad activities, with returns of 250 times the investment and 222 times the investment, respectively. This is not surprising, given the relatively low cost of using an effective referral program as well as web-based marketing to attract increasing numbers of young families. Overall, though, they had an excellent return on investment for this quarter's marketing plan. They had a return of 102 times their investment of $783. Indeed, if they can find additional cost-effective ways to spend more marketing dollars to double the level of prospects calling them, they will grow their enrollment much faster.

Figure 4-2: Tom and Juanita's Return on Investment
by Marketing Effort/Campaign: ABC Learning Center

Marketing Effort	Cost	# of Inquiries	# of Enrollments	Cost Per Inquiry	Cost Per New Cust.	Annual Revenue Generated	ROI
Website/ online ads	$180	20	4	$9	$45	$40,000	222x
Newspaper	$220	2	0	$110	n/a	$0	—
Signage	$75	3	1	$25	$75	$10,000	133x
Community newsletter ad	$100	2	0	$50	n/a	$0	—
Events	$128	8	1	$16	$128	$10,000	78x
Referral program	$80	5	2	$16	$40	$20,000	250x
TOTAL	$783	40	8	$20	$98	$80,000	102x

Also note that the specific code tied to the community newsletter ad did not generate any enrollments. Tom and Juanita initially reacted to the ROI metrics by wanting to discontinue their ad in this particular newsletter and focus more marketing dollars on a sizzling online presence. They agreed, however, that there were other important reasons for continuing to advertise in the community newsletter—it had been a good way to develop partnerships with other local businesses, and they sometimes received free publicity through articles written in the newsletter about their school's events. They decided to keep the ad in the newsletter and continue tracking it over time.

The marketing return on investment metric is yet another example of how information can bring insight, power, and clarity in your business. When you take the time to set up your marketing ROI metrics, you will be rewarded with knowledge that is based in concrete data and that will enable you to make the right decisions about your marketing activities as you grow your enrollment.

5

Retention Rate Metrics

I probably don't have to tell you that two of the biggest costs of your child care program are related to *customer retention*—the proportion of families who stay enrolled with your center from one period to the next (or, the costs associated with marketing and filling your program's open slots)—and *staff turnover*—the proportion of staff members who leave your program from one period to the next (or, the costs associated with finding new employees and hiring them). The most successful child care businesses typically have low levels of customer and staff turnover. So your goal as a child care leader should be to reduce turnover and increase retention of both your customers and your staff. Low rates of customer and staff turnover are critical for your business to achieve optimal financial performance and healthy *operating margins*. *Retention rate metrics* enable you to track your retention and turnover rates of staff and customers so you can work to continuously improve them (that is, lower your turnover and improve your retention) over time.

Customer Retention Rates

The *customer retention rate metric* measures the proportion of families that stay enrolled with your center from one period to the next, usually on an annual basis. The flip side of this metric is *customer turnover*, that is, the proportion of families who leave your center from one period to the next. For example, if you have an average customer retention rate of 80 percent—where eight out of ten customers will remain enrolled during a given time frame—your average customer turnover rate will be 20 percent—where two out of ten customers will leave your program in that same time frame.

When measuring your customer retention rate, you'll want to exclude, or at least account for, the children (or the families of the children, if you're measuring customer retention by family) that simply graduate out of your program because of their age. You want this metric to help you really identify the students or families who are leaving for reasons other than the natural aging-out process, such as moving out of the area, dissatisfaction, job loss, financial hardship, and the like.

Here's how to calculate your customer retention rate. If your child care program had one hundred children enrolled a year ago and today has only ninety of *those same* children (the children who simply graduated out of your program are excluded from the count, as are new children who have enrolled and taken the places of the children who left for reasons other than age-related graduation), then your annual customer retention rate will be 90 percent and, therefore, your annual customer turnover rate will be 10 percent.

At the beginning of each quarter, print and file a list of every child enrolled with you. Doing so will help systemize the process of calculating this metric.

Exercise 4 Calculate Customer Retention Rate and Customer Turnover Rate

Complete this exercise on a quarterly basis for the previous twelve months, and track the results over time.

1. Gather a list of every child enrolled with you today. This is List 1.

2. Gather a list of every child enrolled with you *one year ago* from today. (Cross out or exclude the names of all the children who simply graduated out of the program so that they don't impact the calculation.) This is List 2.

3. Compare List 1 and List 2 and record the number of children who *are* present on List 2 who *are not* present on List 1.   = _____

4. Divide the number recorded in step 3 by the total number of children named on List 2.   = _____

5. Convert your result from line 4 to a percentage by moving the decimal point two places to the right. (For example, if your result is .12, your customer turnover rate is 12 percent.) This is your customer turnover rate.   = _____

6. Compare List 1 and List 2 and record the number of children who are present on both lists. (Exclude those who simply graduated out of the program.)   = _____

7. Divide the number from line 6 by the total number of children named on List 2.   = _____

8. Convert your result from line 7 to a percentage by moving the decimal point two places to the right. (For example, if your result is .85, your customer retention rate is 85 percent.) This is your customer retention rate.   = _____

Staff Retention Rates

The staff retention metric is vitally important, one that's inextricably tied to the quality and well-being of your child care program. *Staff retention* refers to the proportion of staff members who continue working for your program from one period to the next. A high rate of staff turnover is probably an indication that something in your staff management processes needs to be fixed: perhaps you're not hiring the right type of teacher for your program, perhaps your wages and benefits are out of line with your market, or perhaps you have challenges motivating staff over the long term.

I probably don't have to tell you this—staff turnover can be hard on young children, and it's the top reason why many families leave one child care program for another. It's critical that you measure your staff retention rate so you can make fact-based decisions and see the impact of your efforts to continuously improve staff retention over time. Effective child care leaders use staff motivation and appreciation techniques, such as team building, reward systems, and open communication to help teaching staff improve while keeping morale high. As a child care leader, it's your top priority to put these techniques in place to hire and retain good employees. Not only will these efforts result in lower staff turnover, but they'll help you retain strong levels of enrollment.

Print a list of all employees at the beginning of each quarter, and keep it with the rest of your quarterly staff lists in a folder. Doing so will systemize the process of calculating this metric.

Use the following exercise to calculate your staff retention rate.

Exercise 5 Calculate Staff Retention Rate and Staff Turnover Rate

Complete this exercise on a quarterly basis for the previous twelve months, and track the results over time.

1. Gather a list of every person employed with you today. This is List 1.

2. Gather a list of every person employed with you *one year ago* from today. This is List 2.

3. Compare List 1 and List 2 and record the number of employees who *are* present on list 2 who *are not* present on list 1.   = _____

4. Divide the number from step 3 by the total number of staff on List 2.   = _____

5. Convert your result from line 4 to a percentage by moving the decimal point two places to the right. (For example, if your result is .22, your staff turnover rate is 22 percent.) This is your staff turnover rate.   = _____

6. Compare List 1 and List 2 and record the number of employees who are present on both lists.   = _____

7. Divide the number from line 6 by the total number of employees named on List 2.   = _____

8. Convert your result from line 7 to a percentage by moving the decimal point two places to the right. (For example, if your result is .80, your staff retention rate is 80 percent.) This is your staff retention rate.   = _____

Tom and Juanita had a feeling that their staff turnover had taken a turn for the worse over the past twelve months—they had lost two seasoned teachers who had both moved out of the area. They were even more frustrated when, after those teachers left, they had lost four families as well. After they calculated these metrics and saw the results on paper, their feelings were confirmed.

Figure 5-1: Customer and Staff Turnover Rates for ABC Learning Center

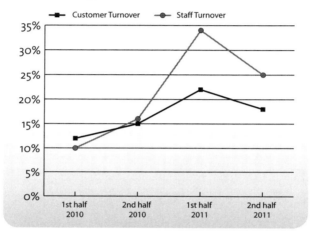

Based on these metrics, Juanita began forming a plan to improve customer and staff retention. She started collecting ideas to build formal customer and staff appreciation programs. She also signed up for some staff motivation and leadership training to get new ideas and skills to manage her staff more effectively.

Retention rate metrics are really a great insight into the health and well-being of your program. If your program has problems such as low staff morale, gossip, lack of motivation, parent dissatisfaction, or other areas of conflict, these metrics will alert and enable you to track the effectiveness (or lack of effectiveness) of your plan to fix the problems. You can also look for statistics in early childhood publications citing industry averages for these metrics to understand how your program compares to other child care centers around your region, state, or industrywide.

Now Take Action!

What follows is a list of everything Tom and Juanita discovered and planned to take action on based on what the nine key metrics told them about their business.

Figure 5-2: ABC Learning Center's New Goals Based on Metrics

Metric	Result	Goals/Action Steps
Lifetime customer value	$25,000 gross	Increase by 10% over the next 12 months to $27,500 through better customer retention
Cost per lead	$20	Increase slightly to cover additional marketing testing and new direct mail
Cost per new customer	$100	Goal is to keep it stable
Raw number of leads (by source)	Avg 10 per month	Double within 90 days to average 20 per month
Conversion ratio of leads to tours	40%	Improve to 50%
Conversion ratio of tours to enrollments	25%	Improve to 35%
ROI of each marketing effort	Varies—not sure because did not track	Track in future by using unique codes and phone numbers for each effort/medium
Customer retention rate	80%	Improve to 90%
Staff retention rate	75%	Improve to 85%

It is extremely important that you, like Tom and Juanita, set up these nine key metrics so you can accurately track the success of your child care center's marketing and enrollment-building efforts. If you don't take time to track these metrics, you'll never know what is working to build your enrollment and what is not.

Employing these nine metrics is the first step in getting really *clear* about how your marketing is working for you and how your enrollment-building efforts are performing. So go ahead. Put down this book and take some action on tracking your metrics right now. Here are some suggested *next steps* to get you started:

☐ Complete the exercises right away, and model the example graphs and charts shown.

☐ Set up a prospect tracking system and train your staff.

☐ Block out chunks of time on your calendar to track these metrics monthly and/or quarterly.

☐ Take a class in Microsoft Excel or other spreadsheet software if you are weak in this area.

☐ Watch for trends and make decisions based on data, not hunches.

☐ Share the information with your staff!

☐ Celebrate if you meet or exceed your goals!

☐ Use the information to promote your center (for example, "Our staff turnover has been reduced by X% this year," or "We have extremely low turnover").

PART

2

Market

Always bear in mind that your own resolution to succeed is more important than any other one thing.

—ABRAHAM LINCOLN

CHAPTER

Know Your Market

The second pillar of an effective marketing plan is your *market*. Your market can be defined as the area where your business is located, as well as the people who live or work there. Depending on the size of your city or town, your market can be a small section of your city or your entire town, a region, or a county. A market is a living, breathing entity, and it's always changing. As your market changes, you must stay on top of what's causing it to change and know how it will affect your business.

Be honest. How well do you really know what's going on in your market? If you can answer most of the following questions, you're doing a good job measuring the pulse of what's happening in your market. If you can't, you have some discovery to do.

Exercise 6 Know Your Market Area

Use the following questions as a guide to discover more about your local market.

1. Which child care programs in your market have the highest rates? What are their rates?

_____

_____

2. Which programs have the lowest rates? What are their rates?

_____

_____

3. Which programs are fully enrolled with a waiting list?

_____

_____

4. Which programs are struggling with enrollment?

_____

_____

5. Which neighborhoods in your market are your program's sweet spots (that is, where do your best customers tend to live)?

_____

_____

6. Which neighborhoods in your market are experiencing growth among young families?

_____

_____

7. Which neighborhoods in your market are declining in growth among young families?

_____

_____

8. How do your rates compare to your competitors' rates?

_____

_____

9. What qualities make your business truly unique in your market?

_____

_____

10. What do your customers like best about your program?

_____

_____

11. What do your customers say is your biggest weakness?

_____

_____

12. What types of child care are in demand right now (for example, second shift, drop-in care)?

_____

_____

If you find yourself unsure of several of the answers in the exercise, don't worry. The chapters in this section of the book will help you discover important and powerful qualities of your market.

When I ask child care leaders to identify the important groups that make up their market, most tell me "families with small children" and "prospective families." I'd like you to go a little deeper than that. Your market is actually composed of five important constituencies: existing customers, prospects, competitors, community partners, and staff. Here's more about each one.

Existing Customers

Current client families (existing customers) are perhaps the most important group in any market. They are the lifeblood of your program, because if they all were to disappear tomorrow, your center would be forced to close. It's vitally important that you connect with, nurture, and leverage your existing customers. Later in the book I'll provide you with effective strategies for connecting and leveraging these relationships.

Prospects

Prospects are parents in your market who are thinking about choosing a child care or preschool program for their young children. Prospects may be expectant parents new to the world of child care or experienced parents considering a switch from one child care program to another. One of the most important functions of a marketing plan is getting your phone to ring. You need a steady stream of prospective customers who are seeking information about your child care program.

Competitors

You may think you know your competitors, but until you've done a complete analysis of their offerings, prices, and marketing messages to determine exactly how your business compares, you may be leaving money on the table.

Here's an example. Perhaps you think your rates are about in the middle of the pack. Then you do a competitive analysis and discover your rates are actually the *lowest* in your market. Based on that information, you decide to raise your rates, significantly boosting your revenue.

While this example is simple and straightforward, many less obvious market opportunities become evident after you spend time researching and analyzing your market.

Community Partners

Community partners can be businesses or organizations that share your target customer. They can also be groups with whom you can share mutual benefits. Examples of potential community partners in your market include pediatric dentists, toy stores, children's clothing stores, consignment shops, family-friendly restaurants, hair salons, local real-estate agents who help young families find housing, elementary school administrators and support staff—even your local ice cream shop! Sometimes spending some time just getting the word out about your child care business to other local shops, businesses, and schools can be enough to build your enrollment to healthy levels.

Staff

Many child care leaders overlook their own staff as a core group of their market. Members of your staff can be a terrific source for referrals, and ideally they're already out in the community saying good things about you! One child care client of mine created a referral program just for her staff. She gave each of her employees personalized business cards, and every time a prospect mentioned a particular staff member as a referral source or produced a staff member's business card, that employee would earn ten referral-reward points. Once an employee reached fifty points (for five referrals), the employee was given a choice—$50 in cash or a gift certificate for a manicure or pedicure.

In each of the next four chapters, we'll learn in much greater detail how to discover more about each of these market segments, as well as strategies for leveraging the relationships you have with these groups to build your enrollment. The four strategies we'll focus on are these:

- Market research: How to gain powerful insights into your core customers by analyzing their geographic and demographic characteristics, and finding the "sweet spot" in your market.
- Your greatest asset: Why your current customers are the biggest asset you have as a business owner, and why most small business owners don't understand or leverage this powerful asset.
- Social proof: Why we rely on our social connections to help us make purchase decisions, whether it's where to eat dinner, what kind of car to buy, or where to place our children in an early childhood program.
- Competitive analysis: How to conduct a competitive analysis in your market, and how to use this valuable information to gain market advantages.

Perhaps the best thing about knowing your market well is the ability it gives you to match your message, your core values, and your media to it. Connecting these things to your market is the basis for developing a highly successful marketing plan and effectively building your enrollment over the long run.

7

Market Research

To better understand the characteristics of your market and what shifts or trends might be taking place, I recommend you spend some time doing core market research. One great way to start is to analyze your current and alumni customer families so you can understand who is and has been attracted to your program.

Geographic and Demographic Profiles

There are two primary profiles of any market: geographic and demographic. A *geographic profile* is the physical location where your market lives or works, and a *demographic profile* is the characteristics that define these constituents, such as income, profession, age, ethnicity, and gender. What follows are some tools you can use to determine the geographic and demographic profiles for your market, as well as information on how to use these profiles to grow your program.

Geographic Profile

Figuring out your geographic profile is pretty straightforward, but don't skip over the following information because you assume you already know it. Keep reading, and I'll demonstrate why.

Your market could be the entire town your business is located in, or that town plus towns that are adjacent to it. Or it could be just the neighborhood in which your business is located. The geographic profile of your market depends on the size of your town or city, whether you're located in a residential or commercial part of town, and the like. For example, if your child care business is in a residential area with few other businesses located nearby, it's likely most of your customers will live within a five-mile radius of your location. On the other hand, if your business is in a commercial or industrial area, you may gain customers because parents with young children work nearby your business.

When I was a new mom, I chose an infant care program across the street from my workplace, which was in a large office park. The majority of this child care program's clientele worked for the same company I did, or they worked for a company located in that same office park. If this is the case for your program, it can be more difficult to reach your target prospects by mailing to their home addresses, for example, because the relationship is based on where they *work* rather than on where they *live*. I will provide some strategies for this type of situation later in this book.

The first step to figuring out the geographic profile of your market is to get a map of your city, town, county, or region. Then gather the home and work addresses of your current and past clientele and plot them on the map. Doing this should show you your market's *sweet spots*—the places where you have a high concentration of customers based on either where they live or where they work. Almost every child care program has sweet spots. Becoming aware of your program's sweet spots is a great strategy for focusing your marketing campaigns. For example, you might use direct mailers and a relationship with your local real-estate agent or Welcome Wagon to set up a meet-and-greet campaign for families just moving in to your sweet spot neighborhoods.

> **TIP:** A great way to use sweet spot data is when you're doing a direct mail campaign. Sweet spot data can help you target families who have young children by zip code or by specific street address. In addition, you can sometimes hire direct mail firms to take your customer list and tell you where your sweet spots are, as opposed to figuring it out yourself with a map.

Do you see how this map-based approach to knowing the geographic profile of your market can help you get really clear about where to find the prospects who have the highest likelihood of enrolling in your program? There are simply going to be certain neighborhoods or commercial areas you can draw prospects from more easily than others.

Now don't forget about the competition! After you've identified your sweet spots, plot your competitors' locations on the same map. Once you have, look over the map. Where is your facility located in relation to your competitors and your existing customers? Do you see any new areas on the map that are a natural fit for your program rather than for your competitors'? For example, if there's a new residential development under construction near your program and you can see that the folks who move into it will have to navigate a busy highway to get to your nearest competitor, this could be a huge competitive advantage for you once those homes are built. On the other hand, if your program is located amid a cluster of competing child care programs, with no clear geographic advantage, you may have to work harder to find a sweet spot to draw from.

One child care business owner I worked with was experiencing a two-year decline in enrollments, which happened to coincide with a new child care center opening on the other side of town. This owner was in denial about the impact the new competing center was having on her enrollments. She'd heard through the grapevine that the program wasn't high quality, and she'd quickly dismissed it as a threat.

But it turns out that this competing program was indeed responsible for a large part of her enrollment decline. Many of the families that had been with her decided to attend the new program because it was located closer to their homes. And because she had failed to market the benefits of her own program to the new families moving into that geographic area, many of them didn't even know about it. This owner had no website and no visibility in the new and growing neighborhoods.

Don't make this mistake! Know the geographic profile of your market, and stay on top of it, because it is dynamic. Take the time to map out your region using the following exercise, and new pockets of opportunity may become clear to you.

Exercise 7 Map It Out

Follow these steps to better understand the geographic profile of—and opportunities within—your market.

1. Get a regional map and lay it out on a large table.
2. Using a highlighter, mark your location on the map.
3. Use a black pen to mark the home address (if your business is residentially located) or work address (if your business is commercially located) of every parent enrolled with you. Consider using a different color pen or even colored push pins to note work versus home addresses.
4. Identify your sweet spots—the neighborhoods and commercial areas that are a natural geographic fit for your program.
5. Mark the location of all your competitors—early childhood programs, preschools, and family child cares homes alike. Your local CCR&R can provide you with a complete listing.
6. Look for new and upcoming pockets of opportunity—new housing developments, new businesses, new construction sites, and so on.

If you're a new child care business owner and yet don't have existing clientele to map out, fear not. Do the mapping exercise anyway to get a handle on the makeup of your geographic location, to look for pockets of enrollment opportunity, and to surmise from where your competitors are probably drawing most of their customers. If you're in start-up mode, the mapping exercise can also help if you haven't yet chosen a location for your new child care program. Look for an area that's not currently being served, or that's underserved compared to the population of young families nearby. Proximity to elementary schools, public playgrounds, churches without a preschool program, and new or growing commercial areas—and, ideally, ample parking!—can provide you with a huge advantage to build enrollment quickly.

Demographic Profile

I can't overstate the importance of knowing the demographic profile of your typical customer if you want to grow your early childhood program. The reasons are many:

- It will save you huge amounts of time and money when you're looking for new prospects to fill open slots.
- It will enable you to place ads in media that will reach your target market.
- It will help you create marketing messages that speak to your customers and prospects with the right message and tone.
- It will provide you with a better understanding of the lives of your clients—you'll be better able to add the right kind of value to your program, value that fits their needs and desires.

TIP: Use online surveys to measure customer satisfaction of parents and prospects alike. They have a higher response rate than printed surveys. Several inexpensive online tools make survey distribution and results compilation a breeze. I recommend one called Survey Monkey (www.surveymonkey.com). A basic account is free and has good functionality.

The best way to figure out your demographic profile is to survey your existing clients. Include questions about demographics on your customer satisfaction survey—which I hope you're conducting at least once a year. Basic demographic information includes the following:

- age of parents
- ethnicity of parents
- number of children they have
- publications they subscribe to
- churches and clubs they belong to
- activities they are involved in

You can also ask for a range of household income.

When you compile the results of your survey, you should be able to summarize the demographic profile of your current clientele. For example, you might see that the majority of your customers are twenty-five to thirty-five years of age, have a household income between $50,000 and $85,000, have two children between the ages of two and six, are of Latino origin, and are predominantly Catholic.

If you're a new child care business owner and don't have existing clientele to survey, again, fear not. Contact your local or regional government offices to find out whether they have demographic surveys or studies of your region that you can use to better learn about the families in your town or city. You might also get some useful demographic information from your local CCR&R, especially if they're keeping track of the characteristics of families who are looking for child care in your area.

The Best Neighborhood Strategy

I first heard about the best neighborhood strategy from sales and marketing expert Chet Holmes (www.chetholmes.com). The *best neighborhood strategy* helps you identify a market sweet spot based on where your best customers and your best prospects live or work so you can aggressively court these folks using direct marketing. Examples of direct marketing include direct mail, door hangers, flyers hung on mailboxes, or even door-to-door visits. Think about it: if month after month you receive an interesting, fun mailer with a special offer from a restaurant near where you live or work, aren't you curious enough to check it out?

Likewise, if you consistently mail a fun, charming, money-saving offer to households with young children in your best neighborhood, then you will almost certainly have prospects from this neighborhood consistently calling about your program. The key is to mail slightly different pieces to

> **TIP:** To send a targeted direct mail campaign to a specific neighborhood, you can consult a direct marketing expert in your area, or you can purchase a mailing list directly from a list broker, such as InfoUSA (www.infousa.com).

your best neighborhood repeatedly—not once, not twice, but every month until they give in and give you a call!

 Tom and Juanita thought they had a pretty good handle on their market—after all, they had owned their center for over fifteen years. However, they had not conducted a survey of their parents in over two years. They decided to use an online survey tool to gather some information about how they were doing to meet their families' needs and to gain some insights into demographics at the same time.

The results of their survey were very enlightening. They found out that their clientele families were split about evenly between Caucasian and Hispanic or Latino ethnicity, and most of the parents were ages thirty to forty. They had household incomes of $75,000 to $125,000 on average, which was a little higher than Tom and Juanita thought.

On the geographic side, Tom and Juanita used the mapping exercise, which indicated that most of their families lived within a three-mile radius of their school, and that two core neighborhoods provided 65 percent of their clientele. So Tom and Juanita are now able to be *much* more targeted (and in turn, much more cost effective) in their efforts to directly market to new prospects. Knowing these demographic and geographic profiles allowed them to purchase a list of similar parents from their direct mail vendor and also to target *new* families moving into their key neighborhoods.

Again, when you know more about the lives of your clients, you'll be able to reach them much more effectively and add the right kind of value to your program to meet their needs and desires. Now let's discover why your current customers are not only the lifeblood of your child care program, but also the greatest asset you have as a business owner.

8

Your Greatest Asset

When I ask child care leaders and owners to name their business's greatest asset, they often answer, "Our program," or "Our staff," or "Our facility." Guess what? These responses are all off the mark. For a child care business—for any small business—*current customers* are its greatest asset. They offer a tremendous opportunity to get more revenue flowing into your child care program. Dennis Vicars, a child care management expert, says, "Offer a superior product to my child, delivered to me as a parent in a way that makes me a partner in the process, and I will be your greatest advocate and tell the world" (*Exchange Magazine,* May/June 2011, 78).

Most small business advisers agree that it's usually easier to get more revenue from people already doing business with you than it is to get new customers. And while many small business owners are aware of this, they tend to ignore it. They simply do not take the time to figure out how to maximize their greatest asset—their existing customers—and increase their lifetime customer value.

Three primary strategies can maximize the value of current customers and bring in more revenue:

- Extend the client relationship by adding new programs.
- Offer complementary, value-added services.
- Offer "wow" experiences that turn customer goodwill into a stream of prospects through word-of-mouth promotion.

Let's talk about each strategy in more detail.

Extend the Client Relationship by Adding New Programs

Perhaps the most obvious way to maximize current customer relationships and increase your lifetime customer value is to extend the length of time families stay enrolled with you. You can do this by extending your care to school-age children, establishing before-school and after-school care, a full-service summer camp for older children, or even a full-day private kindergarten or elementary school. One child care program I work with has had great success offering a full-time summer camp with weekly field trips to outdoor pools and lakes. Many of the families whose children no longer attend the early childhood program during the school year sign their children up for this popular, alumni-targeted summertime opportunity.

Offer Complementary Value-Added Services

Another way to increase your revenue per existing family is to add services that complement your core offerings. Ideas for this include offering the following:

- birthday parties
- craft parties
- mommy-and-me yoga on weekends or weeknights
- tutoring
- dance lessons
- art lessons
- drama classes
- music lessons (especially if you have a piano in your school)

You can outsource these additional services through an external service provider and then split the revenues, and you can extend the additional services to the public to attract new clients. Offer a special members' price to your enrolled families that is lower than the nonmembers' price paid by the general public. When you do this, the additional services will be seen as a benefit to using your early childhood care.

You can also offer services that busy parents often need, such as on-site haircuts for children, fully prepared dinners that just need to be reheated, dry-cleaning drop-off and pickup, and the like. Again, you can partner with local businesses that provide these kinds of services and create a joint partnership where you receive a commission for each new customer you bring them. In return they would promote your business to their clientele.

Offer "Wow" Experiences That Turn Customer Goodwill into a Stream of Prospects

The third big way to gain more revenue from existing clients is to simply provide them with unsurpassed "wow" experiences that literally *compel* them to rave about you to their neighbors, family members, friends, and coworkers. "Wow" ideas include customer appreciation events, thank-you gifts, parent advisory boards, or out-of-the-ordinary field trips or experiences for their child.

Here are just a few examples of actual "wow" experiences I've seen child care business owners implement with great success:

- Mail a birthday card to each enrolled child, signed by the owner, director, and teacher.
- Mail an anniversary card to the parents.
- Give birthday or anniversary gifts or experiences (for example, complimentary child care and a $50 gift card to a restaurant).
- Provide parents with fresh gourmet coffee in a to-go coffee mug with the center's logo on the mug every morning.
- Offer chair massages for parents at the end of the day. (Yes, this has actually been done!)
- Offer free weekend or evening mommy-and-me yoga classes.
- Organize a pet parade (families can bring their pets to the park for a parade).
- On the anniversary of their start date, give special recognition and a gift to families who have been enrolled for two, three, or five years or more. (When other parents hear about this, they will calculate how much longer they have to wait till they get recognized—especially if the gift is a really good one!)

Of course, costs can be associated with offering these "wow" experiences, although many of the ideas listed above are very low cost. From what I've seen, the benefits of implementing these ideas vastly outweigh the expense. For example, I know an owner who hosted a Parent Appreciation Day with snacks, gifts, and chair massages; she spent about $500 on the event. The value of the rave reviews, enhanced parent relationships, and additional referrals she received as a result of the event, however, greatly exceeded the $500 expense. In other words, by implementing these ideas and boosting levels of satisfaction and word-of-mouth promotion among your parent clientele, you are likely to receive a tremendous return on your investment.

Not only are your existing customers the most important factor in your *current* enrollment revenues—they are the most important factor in your *future* enrollment revenues. Every loyal and satisfied customer has a huge positive impact on your business above and beyond the money they pay for your services. A satisfied customer potentially can tell dozens and dozens of people about your business. As Dennis Vicars said, a satisfied customer can *tell the world*. (Methods for leveraging word-of-mouth promotion through testimonials and referrals will be discussed in the next chapter.)

Because current customers are your greatest asset, it's important to spend some time developing a plan to improve their satisfaction with your program and to strengthen their loyalty to it. I'll provide you with strategies and guidance for developing this customer satisfaction and loyalty plan throughout the rest of this chapter.

Improve Customer Satisfaction

Allow me to back up a bit and discuss a core principle for being a good business owner or manager. No matter how good your marketing is, or how many "wow" factors you have in your program, it's going to be an uphill battle if you have lousy customer service and poor customer satisfaction. It's up to you to keep the parents and the children in your program happy so they'll stay enrolled and tell other families about what a great job you do. Two of the best methods for improving and maintaining high levels of customer satisfaction are daily relationship-building and developing solid two-way communication.

Build Relationships Every Day

Unlike almost any other service business in the world, early childhood providers have a unique opportunity: they get to meet and greet their customers every day, twice a day. Think about other service businesses—dry cleaners, real estate agents, doctors, dentists, cleaning services, and restaurants. Not one of them gets to see and greet each of their customers every day.

This huge opportunity to build a close-knit rapport with customers is often overlooked by child care business owners and directors. Let me share a real-world "wow" example.

Several child care businesses I work with implemented an idea of mine to set up a coffee station for their parents. Every morning when parents would drop off their children, they could take a to-go cup of free hot coffee—and occasionally a donut or a bagel—in with them. This may not seem like something parents would rave about, but it was. The programs that implemented the idea got rave reviews from parents, many of whom went on to tell their coworkers, friends, and neighbors how happy they were that their child care program provided them with a cup of coffee every day.

Do you think these businesses strengthened relationships with their current customers when they provided this coffee service? Yes, they did! Do you think the strengthened relationships helped improve customer satisfaction? Without a doubt! And do you think this improved customer satisfaction resulted in new clients for the program? Absolutely! And at a lifetime customer value of $25,000 per enrolling family, do you think it was a worthwhile investment to spend $75 each week on coffee and to-go cups? Again, absolutely! This one idea illustrates that a child care business benefits greatly from finding creative ways to strengthen the bonds with families.

Develop Strong Two-Way Communication with Parents

You and your staff simply cannot communicate too frequently with your parent-clients. After all, how many parents do you know who get tired of hearing feedback about their children? In fact, when I talk to parents from around the country whose children are in child care programs, one of the biggest reasons they give for leaving a particular program is *lack of communication* from the program's caregivers and directors. I'm not talking about random chit-chat, but rather a systematic way to foster two-way communication with families. You and your staff need to provide high-quality communication to parents about what happens in their child's day every day.

Here are some fresh ideas for taking your daily communication with parents to the next level. Consider using these strategies to add some "oomph" to typical methods of communicating:

Daily feedback forms. Many of you already use daily feedback forms, which are a great way to communicate with parents. Every now and then, consider making small changes to the way the form looks or the information it relates to keep it fresh. Add a twist when you can. For instance, include something like, "Max's favorite activity today was _____," or "A special thing Emily did today was _____." When my daughter was in preschool, her daily form included the letter, shape, number, and color of the day. On our drive home, we would play a quiz game to see if she could recall each item. This ritual helped me engage with her and share in her day, and my daughter really seemed to enjoy and value the routine and the connection it forged too.

Parent-teacher conferences. Most early childhood programs schedule regular parent-teacher conferences. Look for ways to add pizzazz and to leverage them into relationship-building sessions. For instance, you could add a ten-minute "Director-Parent" meeting at the end of each conference, where the director checks in with parents one-on-one. You could ask the children to do a special conference-time art project for the teachers to give to parents as a surprise at the end of the meeting as an extra loving touch.

Newsletters. You should create and distribute parent newsletters every two months at a minimum; a monthly newsletter is even better. Send them electronically via e-mail—a great way to save paper and be green—or print them and mail them to the homes of your families. Don't put newsletters out on the counter at the front desk for parents to take on their own or put them into the children's cubbies—sure ways to reduce readership. Leverage your newsletter into a relationship-building vehicle by including monthly columns, such as "Family of the Month," "A Q&A from Our Parents," "Rave Review of the Month," or "Funny Quotes from the Children." Look for creative ways to use your newsletter to build rapport with parents and enhance their sense of community. Make it fun to read, even wacky at times, and readership will increase.

E-mail and website updates. Ask parents how they prefer to get news and updates from you. These days many prefer getting electronic rather than printed information. It's a good idea to collect every parent's e-mail contact information using an Outlook address book or, even better, an e-mail broadcast tool like Constant Contact (learn more at www.constantcontact.com). Then, once or twice a week, send brief updates, news, or photos—whatever you think your parent clients will appreciate receiving.

Facebook and Twitter. Because Facebook can be a great place to strengthen bonds with parents as well as find new prospective families for your program, I recommend setting up a Facebook page (also known as a fan page) for your child care program. Once you do, be sure to send all your parents and prospects an e-mail containing the link to your program's fan page, and tell them they can become a fan by clicking the "Like" button.

If you are active on Twitter, you or a designated staff member who enjoys "tweeting" can handle the job of posting updates to your followers. And don't forget to add links from your website home page to your Facebook and Twitter pages. (For more information on social media, see chapter 17.)

A note of caution regarding Facebook: be sure to get parental approval to use any child's photo on your Facebook page or website. Many parents are understandably nervous about having their child's photo posted online.

Surveys. I recommend doing parent satisfaction surveys of existing clients at least once each year, but preferably every six months. As I mentioned earlier, the online survey tool SurveyMonkey works really well. See appendix B for a sample parent survey you can model.

Remember, though, that if you ask parents to tell you what top improvement you could make to your program, you must take action when they respond. And once you have, you can circle back to let them know what you did, and that you did it based on their input. This will demonstrate that you're listening to their suggestions and create a sense of partnership and buy-in.

Live events. Special events for your families are a fabulous way to build relationships and strengthen bonds with parents. Popular special events include Mom's Night Out, Grandparents Lunch, Donuts with Dad, Taco Tuesday Nights for families, and field trips for the whole family. When they participate in special events, families in your program also get to know each other better, which makes the likelihood that they'll stay enrolled with you that much higher.

Communication with parents is vital to the growth and financial well-being of your program. Use the following exercise to improve and strengthen your customer relationships by creating a communication plan.

Exercise 8 Create a Parent Communication Plan

Write out specific methods and strategies you and your staff will use over the next twelve months to improve and strengthen communications with parents, such as monthly newsletters, e-mail blasts, daily two-way communication methods, and parent-teacher conferences. Use the open lines below to note your specific methods and ideas. Make a communications plan for the year. Engage your staff, and have fun with it!

1. Daily feedback forms: _____

   _____

   _____

2. Parent-teacher conferences: _____

   _____

   _____

3. Newsletters: _____

   _____

   _____

4. E-mail and website communication: _____

   _____

   _____

5. Social media: _____

_____

_____

6. Surveys and contests: _____

_____

_____

7. Live events: _____

_____

_____

8. Other ideas: _____

_____

_____

Strengthen Customer Loyalty

I like to use the term *loyalty fence* to define the strength of your bond with your customer families. The more you do to build a loyalty fence around your customers, the harder it will be for your competitors to woo them away. The more loyal your customers feel toward your program, the more likely they will be to recommend it to others. And if your relationship with parents is built on a foundation of loyalty, trust, and goodwill, parents will be much less likely to leave your program should minor incidents or misunderstandings occur.

With that in mind, here are a few strategies you can implement to strengthen your loyalty fence:

Holiday events. If your program participates in and organizes holiday festivities throughout the year—for instance, a neighborhood caroling outing for parents and children during the holiday season, or an Earth Day festival where each family plants a tree together—your program will make an indelible stamp on the memories of your customer families. With a fresh set of eyes, look at the holiday events your program offers and strive to take them up a notch. Play up fun holidays like Halloween, Valentine's Day, St. Patrick's Day, and the Fourth of July.

Customer appreciation events. The goal of a customer appreciation event is to create an irresistible urge among your parent-clients to rave about your program to their friends, coworkers, and neighbors. You can and should do customer appreciation events for the whole family, children included, as well as for just the parents. Offer a complimentary parents' night out event two or three times a year. Parents will perceive the service as a tremendous value, though there won't be much cost for you. Also, host a family night or open house where the whole family can come in for a reading and pajama party, arts and crafts night, movie night, and so on.

Parent board. An excellent way to demonstrate that you value parents is to hold a monthly parent board meeting. Begin the meeting when your center closes for the evening, around 6:30, and provide child care for thirty or forty-five minutes while you, administrative staff, and parents get together to map out future improvements to the program. Provide a light dinner like pizza and a salad for everyone—a great added touch. A parent board fosters buy-in among your parent-clients, making them feel they're a partner in determining the future of your child care program.

Parent volunteers. Don't hesitate to ask a parent to volunteer when you need help with a special project, like planning and planting a children's garden or freshening up your website. Parents who volunteer their skills are especially likely to bring you referrals. They know they're adding value to your program, and they feel like part of the family because of it. A great volunteer idea for the really busy parent is to have him come in and read his favorite children's book to his child's class.

When you implement even a few loyalty-building ideas, your relationship with parent-clients will become more solid. Your lifetime customer value will increase as families stay with you longer, and your enrollment will grow as parents rave about you to their friends, family members, and colleagues.

Exercise 9 Create a Parent Appreciation and Loyalty-Building Plan

Write out specific methods and strategies you and your staff will use over the next twelve months to demonstrate that you appreciate your customer families.

1. Make a list of everything you are currently doing in your program to build relationships with parents and show them special appreciation.

2. Obtain or create a calendar of the next twelve months. (You can do a paper version, or draw it out on a large whiteboard.) On it, record the dates of all the events and efforts you are doing that relate to customer appreciation and loyalty-building. (Though some events may not be planned for the purpose of customer appreciation, you can fairly easily add an element of family fun to an event to draw in existing families and make them feel extra special. For example, you might plan a special series of events for parents and prospects in late February and early March to celebrate Dr. Seuss's birthday.)

3. Determine and list all the tasks that must happen in advance of each event or special date to help you plan to make the event a success.

4. Decide who you can delegate these tasks to.

5. Follow up on each task to make sure it is completed on time.

 In the last chapter, we learned that Tom and Juanita have a fairly even mix of white and Hispanic or Latino families in their program, so they decided it would be fun to celebrate their diversity. They conducted a brief verbal poll of their parent clientele and determined that most of them thought the idea of having a Culture Fair was fantastic—this would be a way to celebrate the traditions, food, music, and culture of all the families in the program. Based on the success of the Culture Fair, Tom and Juanita also started incorporating cross-cultural photos, family stories, and children's artwork into their child care center communications plan. They made this aspect of their program a major theme; it even became a unique difference that they could market to prospective parents who were looking for a diverse and globally oriented early childhood program. Best of all, the children enjoyed learning each other's languages, traditions, and cultures. Tom and Juanita used the ideas of a Parent Communications Plan and a Parent Appreciation/Loyalty-Building Plan to strengthen bonds with their families. They continued to communicate with them and stay in touch after the children left their program so they could celebrate their successes as elementary school children and adolescents.

Remember, your current customer families are the most important asset of your child care business because they have a massive impact on your business above and beyond the money they pay for your services. They have the potential of telling dozens and dozens of people about your business. Perhaps your most important job as a child care owner or director is to keep current customers happy by constantly looking for ways to improve customer satisfaction and strengthen customer loyalty.

Social Proof

Have you ever heard the term *social proof*? Social proof is like word-of-mouth advertising but far more powerful. Social proof can be anything that makes you believe a particular product or service really works, really delivers on its promise. Social proof credibly demonstrates the benefits of a product or service. One of the most powerful forms of social proof is the testimonial—a rave review based on one person's experience with a product or service.

Case in point: You go to your neighborhood holiday party, and your neighbor shows up twenty pounds lighter. She tells you about the amazing new diet she's been following, and she gushes about how easy it was to lose the weight. Now, if you want to shed a few pounds, there's a strong likelihood you'll give her new diet a try, based simply on what she shared with you about her experience. You may even go home that very night, get on the computer, and purchase whatever products she said she used. (Don't deny it—you know it's true!)

This is social proof. Can you see its power?

Testimonials

One of the strongest forms of social proof is the *testimonial*. If we see a product or service that features lots of believable testimonials from real people who talk and look like us, we're much more likely to buy it. Testimonials are social proof that something really works, and they can help consumers overcome any skepticism they may feel. Testimonials from your current customers are a simple, massive weapon in your marketing arsenal, and you simply cannot overuse them.

Most child care businesses I work with, however, aren't using testimonials enough: they may have a couple posted on their website or printed in a brochure; many are not using them at all! Customer testimonials are a source of marketing power in your child care business because they offer crucial social proof to prospective customers that you provide a quality child care experience. What other people have to say about your program is more powerful than anything you can say about yourself. In fact, many marketing experts agree that credible testimonials are up to ten times more believable than marketing claims made by the company itself.

Strategies for Powerful Testimonials

When I talk about using testimonials to provide social proof for your child care business, I'm not talking about just a few quotes simply scattered here and there on your website or in a brochure. You must have a strategic system in place for gathering a multitude of testimonials that contain the messages you need consumers to hear to get new enrollments. Your testimonial system needs to address these factors:

Quantity. Simply put, you can never have too many testimonials. When prospective families look at your marketing materials, they should be blown away by the number of people saying great things about you. Ideally you would have one great testimonial on every page on your website plus an additional page that's nothing but testimonials (five or six high-quality ones at a minimum). More is always better.

Quality. You want testimonials that mention specific benefits of your program, such as "The caregivers helped my child overcome a behavioral issue," or "The teachers were directly responsible for preparing my child to excel in kindergarten." Benefit-driven testimonials that demonstrate the results or outcomes your product or service provide are much stronger than generic ones, such as "This center provides great child care."

Variety. It's also good to include testimonials that address possible objections prospective customers may have to your program. Identify your program's biggest weakness and use a testimonial to diffuse it. For example, if your facility is an older one, find a testimonial that says something like, "The facility may be older than the new franchise across town, but the quality of care is superb, and my children's development is more important to me than a new building."

Identity. I recommend you use only testimonials of people who have given you permission to use their full name, the town they live in, and if possible, the name and age of their child. That way, the signature line after the testimonial would read something like, "Margaret Jones, Springfield, Ohio—Mom of Jason, age 2." You can obtain this permission by adding a sentence at the end of your testimonial request form that says something like, "I authorize the use of this testimonial on all marketing materials, including my name, my town, and my children's names." Including this information makes the testimonial more believable and credible. An additional touch is to ask the parent to provide a photo for you to use with the testimonial.

Multimedia. One of the most powerful ways to use testimonials is to add an audio or video component. For example, you can feature video testimonials on your website or compile them on a DVD to send to prospects in the mail. An inexpensive and easy way to add audio testimonials to your website is a service called AudioAcrobat, which stores your audio testimonials for a small

TIP: A good way to host audio on your website is to use an affordable service called Audio-Acrobat. You can have your parents record testimonials using AudioAcrobat; the service will host the audio and link it to your website for one low monthly fee. It's supereasy! For more information, visit www .audioacrobat.com.

TIP: You don't need an expensive or complicated video camera to gather Internet-quality video testimonials. Many smartphones are equipped with video cameras that are easy to use. You can also purchase small, user-friendly, portable video cameras for less than $200.

monthly fee. (See sidebar for contact information.) Your customers simply call a toll-free number that's been set up just for you and record their testimonials over the phone. The testimonial is saved for you, and you receive a link to add to your website. Video testimonials are even more powerful than audio ones and can be captured and uploaded easily using a small video camera.

Here are two sample testimonials. Which one do you think would be more credible to prospective customers and effective at bringing new leads to a child care program?

Testimonial A

"My daughter and I love this school! The teachers are wonderful."
—Susan S.

Testimonial B

"To say that we are pleased with the care our children have received at ABC Learning Center would be a huge understatement. Our children have *thrived* as a result of being with teachers who are truly devoted to creating a fun environment of learning for *each and every child* in their classroom. Moreover, the staff is genuinely interested in the over-all well-being of our children, and they went above and beyond to make sure we knew how much they would love to care for our young-est daughter, who has special needs. Since starting at ABC, Eva has made remarkable progress, and we attribute her recent milestones to her wonderful teachers. Their guidance and encouragement have been invaluable. *Sending our children to ABC has been one of the best decisions we've ever made.*"
—Susan and John Smithson, Hudson, New York
(parents of Owen, 7; Sarah, 4; and Eva, 15 months)

I hope you chose testimonial B! As you can see, by giving the full name of the parent, the names and ages of the children, specific examples of how the pro-gram improved the lives of this family, and a photo of the parent, your testimonial will be much more believable. Testimonial B is much stronger—powerful social proof that your program is excellent!

Generating Testimonials

You need to have a strategy for generating a multitude of testimonials. A great way to generate them is to hold a testimonial contest. Create a print or electronic flyer about the contest to send to your parent-clients. Be sure to set a deadline for turning in the testimonials, and remind parents of the deadline by e-mail or in a newsletter. Tell parents that the best testimonial received will win a valuable prize. Or choose the winning testimonial by drawing it from among all the testimonials submitted—and again, the winner will receive a valuable prize. The prize should be something that gets people excited enough to take action: dinner for two plus free child care, a day at the spa, or a $200 gift card might do the trick. (Remember, by gathering lots of great testimonials, you are investing in one of the best ways to consistently build your enrollment, so your expenditure will be well worth it.)

Once the winning testimonial has been selected, take a photo of the parent who provided it holding the prize. Ideally, everyone who provides a testimonial would receive a small gift, such as a $5 gift card to a local coffee shop or some other treat. At the very least, each participant should receive a simple thank-you note.

The best time to get a testimonial from a parent is right after you receive some positive feedback from her. Simply say, "Hey, thanks so much for your great feedback! Would you mind if I paraphrase your comment and create a testimonial from it? I'll run it by you to get your permission after I've written it up." Or hand her a form you've created in advance and ask her if she'd mind jotting down her comments in a quick testimonial for you. You'll be surprised how happy people are to do this. You just need to start asking!

Figure 9-1: Sample Testimonial Contest Form

TESTIMONIAL CONTEST ENTRY FORM
ABC LEARNING CENTER

Thanks for providing a customer review for our child care program! All testimonials received by Friday, January 21, will be entered into a random drawing for a really great prize! We appreciate your feedback, and we look forward to creating happy memories with your child throughout the coming year and beyond!

—Tom and Juanita, ABC Learning Center

Name: _____

Occupation: _____

Number of years as our client: _____

Describe the one or two most important benefits your family has received from our

program. Please be as specific as possible. _____

_____

What do you value most about our program? _____

_____

What does your child love most about our program? _____

_____

By signing below, you give us permission to use your name and comments in any or all of our promotional materials.

Signature: _____

Date: _____

Please return this form before the contest deadline: Friday, January 21.

Bring the form to our office, fax it to us, or scan and e-mail it to us. Thank you!

Juanita and Tom attended a child care conference and had heard positive stories from several of their colleagues who were using testimonials in very creative ways to build enrollment. Sally, one of these colleagues, had even enlarged her best parent testimonials on poster board, framed them, and hung them in the hallways of her center. When she gave tours to prospects, they always commented on the "rave reviews" of her program. Sally even had a framed testimonial hanging in the parent restroom! This was a subtle but highly effective idea that Tom and Juanita acted on when they returned from the conference. They also made sure their website had lots of glowing testimonials and checked their parent reviews at online websites such as Google to make sure their program was being seen in a positive light online.

Referral-Rewards Programs

Joe Girard, author of *How to Sell Anything to Anybody*, contends that each customer a business markets to has the potential to refer on average fifty-two new customers to that business. Even when we cut Girard's number in half, ask yourself: Does your child care program receive an average of twenty-six referrals per customer? Word of mouth is the most powerful form of advertising. Why, then, don't more early childhood programs reward customers who refer others to them?

The fastest way to double your enrollment is to get each of your current customers to refer just one family who enrolls to your program. It's important to reward existing customers for their referrals; unless you reward them, existing customers are unlikely to help you get many new ones. They may refer a few people here and there, but without a reward for the time and effort they spend to refer you to their friends, family, neighbors, and colleagues, they're unlikely to feel motivated. It's important to create a referral culture in your child care business.

The simplest, easiest way to create a customer *referral-rewards program* is to follow a simple three-step acronym, EAR (earn, ask, and reward):

Earn. Do what you do so well that customers won't be able to *resist* telling others about you. If you want parents to rave about your program, you have to provide them with a "wow" experience! Ask yourself how you can provide child care services so excellent that parents will want to tell others about them. Make a list of what's special and unique about your program. When prospects call and then visit for the first time, what "wow" reactions do you think they'll have? If prospects were to visit you and two of your competitors in the same day, what would make them prefer your program to the other two? Don't let your prospects have a ho-hum experience.

Ask. You simply must ask customers to refer your program to prospects. The perfect moment to ask a customer for a referral is when he compliments something about your staff or your program. Remind him of your rewards program, and ask him to do you a favor by mentioning his great experience with your program to coworkers, friends, and neighbors. Set a goal to verbally ask two customers each month for referrals, and increase that number over time. When you do, you'll start getting a steady stream of referred customers to your child care program.

Reward. Give something that will be meaningful to your customers. This is not the time to be cheap—remember the lifetime customer value of a typical family to your center's revenue. You can give a $300 reward for each referral that ends up in an enrollment and still be highly profitable. Consider giving something tangible rather than, for example, a tuition discount. One of the best gifts you can give to parents is a complimentary date night that includes dinner and a movie for two and free child care for the evening.

I recommend you establish an easy step-by-step procedure for you and your staff to follow when asking happy customers to refer your program. Do this by creating a procedure for your staff to follow and a simple flyer for parents and prospects that spells out the details of your child care referral-rewards program and includes information about the reward. The following exercise will help you get started.

Exercise 10 Create a Customer Referral-Rewards Program (EAR)

The following questions are designed to help you create a referral-rewards program for your child care business. Answering them will enable you to think creatively about how to optimize this kind of program for your unique situation.

1. How can you provide child care services so excellent that parents will want to tell others about them?

    _____

    _____

    _____

2. List the special and unique qualities of your program.

    _____

    _____

    _____

3. When prospects call and then visit for the first time, what "wow" reactions will they have?

    _____

    _____

4. If prospects were to visit you and two of your competitors in the same day, what would make them prefer your program to the other two?

    _____

    _____

    _____

5. When a customer compliments your program, what would you say in response to encourage him to provide a referral?

    _____

    _____

    _____

6. List ideas for good referral rewards.

_____

_____

_____

The referral reward is typically given when the enrolling family names the referring family. For example, on your enrollment form you should have a field stating, "Please let us know who referred you to our program so that we may thank them." Spread the word by talking up your referral program in all of your marketing materials—your newsletter, e-mail correspondence, website home page, and parent bulletins posted on the parent communication board.

Alumni Families

In addition to current customers, you can use the EAR referral-reward program with past customers—alumni families—who have successfully graduated out of your early childhood program. One great way to stay in contact with alumni families is to keep them on your e-mail list or direct mailing list, and send them your program newsletter on a regular basis. Then you can simply let them know about your new referral-rewards program and how it can benefit them as well as current customers. At the same time, engage with alumni parents by discovering what honors, awards, or achievements in sports or other areas their children have accomplished recently so that you can communicate these newsworthy alumni accomplishments on a "What are they up to now?" board in the main hallway of your facility. Doing this reinforces the notion that your program is high quality and valuable, and it's an effective enrollment tool to use during a tour with prospects.

In addition to current customers and alumni, two more groups you can draw into the referral-rewards program are community partners and staff.

Community Partners

Community partners are other local businesses that share your ideal customer. As mentioned earlier in this book, good community partners for an early child care business include toy stores, children's clothing stores and consignment shops, family and children's hair salons, pediatricians, pediatric dentists, and real-estate agents who serve young families moving into the area.

The goal of working with community partners is to set up reciprocal-referral relationships to create a system for referring one another to current and prospective customers. If you can establish effective referral relationships, you might end up with ten or twenty businesses in your community sending a constant stream of leads your way. If in a month you can get ten new business partners on board, and they refer five people each to your program, that's fifty new leads in one month!

Here are four steps for creating a community partner referral-rewards program for your child care business—and for getting people in your community to promote you like crazy!

Step 1: Identify who in your market has access to your ideal customer. Ideally, you and your community partners will share a very similar client profile, such as parents with young children who match your client demographic-geographic profile. Make a list of your ideal community partners and prepare to approach them as potential referral partners. Consider including on the list newly established business owners, who are typically eager to work with others willing to help them get their word out.

Step 2: Write a letter to your potential referral partners describing your reciprocal-referral partner program. Print as many letters as you'll need to approach each of your potential partners. Consider attaching the letter to your program's brochure to provide more information to the business owners about who you are.

Figure 9-2: Sample Reciprocal-Referral Partner Program Letter

Dear Springfield Business Owner,

ABC Learning Center is actively building enrollment through our new **reciprocal-referral partner program**. Simply put, ABC will display **your promotional materials** and refer your family-friendly business to our existing customer base of seventy-five Springfield-area families. In exchange, we ask that you keep our marketing materials on display at your business and refer our high-quality child care, preschool, and kindergarten programs to families when appropriate.

If you are interested in a **mutually beneficial reciprocal-referral relationship** with us, please contact our marketing representative, Kris Murray, at 330-555-1315. Kris will provide you with our materials and pick up whatever materials you would like displayed at ABC. When you run out of our materials, please call or e-mail Kris at kris@childcare-marketing .com to restock.

We would like to schedule a brief phone call with you to discuss other cross-promotional opportunities, such as reciprocal links between our websites, cobranded promotions and ads, and offers from your business for our parent goodie bags. We will call you early next week to set up a time to talk.

Thank you so much. We look forward to sending **more customers** to your business!

Best regards,
Tom and Juanita, Owners
ABC Learning Center

Step 3: Journey out into your community. Make a visit to each potential referral partner on your list. When you arrive, introduce yourself to the employee who first receives you, and ask to speak to the owner. If the owner isn't available, explain your program briefly to the employee and ask him to give your letter and materials to the owner. If you do speak directly to the owner, be sure to emphasize that you'll be promoting her business to your clients as well; give her the "what's in it for her." Remember to get the business card or name of the owner so you can follow up appropriately.

Step 4: Follow up! This is the critical step. Within five days of your initial visit, follow up with each one of the business owners on your list. Preferably, this follow-up would be done in person, but you can also try following up by telephone or e-mail to see whether it's effective. Give each business that agrees to participate in your community partner referral program twenty-five to fifty brochures, flyers, or postcards to display in a public area at their business. Include in your promotional material a special offer to prospective customers and a deadline for taking action. You want to intrigue prospects with a deadline-driven, irresistible offer that will make them pick up the phone and call or drop by your facility; your brochure alone won't be enough. Be sure to include a unique offer code on the special offer to measure the effectiveness of your community efforts. When you do, you'll be able to track how many leads and then enrollments you're getting from the community referral program, and then determine your marketing return on investment.

Be sure to collect promotional materials from your community referral partners and let them know you're actively displaying their materials and promoting their businesses. Create a display in a community area of your child care facility with a dozen or so brochures, postcards, or flyers. Touch base with your referral partners at least once a month to see whether they need you to replenish your materials or provide additional information.

Exercise 11 Establish Community Referral Partners

This exercise will help you create a framework for your community referral partner program. Complete the following steps to get started.

1. Identify and make a list of ten to twenty businesses in your market that have access to your ideal customer.

   _____   _____

   _____   _____

   _____   _____

   _____   _____

_____ _____

_____ _____

_____ _____

_____ _____

_____ _____

_____ _____

2. List three to five benefits of the reciprocal-referral partner program to include in your letter to potential partners.

_____

_____

_____

_____

3. Write out a brief introduction of yourself and your objective to use when meeting potential partners in your community.

_____

_____

_____

_____

4. Record the dates on which you plan to visit a potential partner, as well as the follow-up dates if you're unable to speak to the business owner.

_____ _____

_____ _____

_____ _____

_____ _____

Employees

The final group you can reward for referrals is your staff. It's sometimes easy to overlook employees as a potential referral source, but after all, they are (you hope) the people out in the community who sing your program's praises the most. What better way to leverage this positive PR than to establish a referral-rewards programs for employees too? An easy way to do this is to provide every employee with personalized business cards that they can hand out to friends, neighbors, and acquaintances as they talk about where they work. When a prospective customer mentions that an employee referred her to your program, or she produces that employee's business card for you during the tour, you can reward the employee for bringing in the lead.

One option is to create a points-based tracking system. For example, each referral earns an employee ten points. Once an employee reaches fifty points (or five referrals in this case), she would get a gift, such as an extra paid vacation day, a manicure/pedicure gift certificate, or even cash. Ask your employees what they'd most like to receive, and offer those things as rewards. Whatever you choose, your staff rewards program can boost morale and even improve staff retention by making your staff feel like they are part of your team as you all work together toward a common goal: a fully enrolled program.

 Tom and Juanita made a plan for getting more referrals from their community partners. They had a great relationship with a local pediatric dentist; they started receiving a couple of referrals each month from this dentist after putting their reciprocal-referral program in place. They discovered another interesting thing too—a local real-estate agent, a specialist in helping young Hispanic professionals relocate to their town, had been referring their program. (Tom and Juanita discovered this when they conducted their customer survey and two of their current clients mentioned being referred by this particular real-estate agent). They sent a gift basket of fruit and chocolates to this real-estate agent and followed up with a phone meeting. They were able to strengthen their relationship with the real-estate agent and made some connections for future referrals. Tom and Juanita were excited to see their enrollment growing and were feeling confident about having marketing strategies that were working!

I hope you can see the tremendous impact that testimonials and referrals can have on building your enrollment. I recommend that you begin using these strategies right away to get more social proof about how great your early childhood program is. You'll see a dramatic difference in your enrollment once you start using testimonials and referrals effectively and more often, along with help from your current customer base, alumni families, community partners, and staff.

10

Competitive Analysis

We talked earlier about mapping out your market, which included identifying and locating all of your competitors. Identifying your competition is the first step in analyzing the competition in your market. Now it's time to take the second step: getting really clear about the strengths and weaknesses of your competition. Based on your ongoing competitive analyses, you will gain valuable insights about how to adapt or to build your child care business to carve out your own unique market niche.

You'll want to discover some key pieces of information about your competitors. Start by compiling the following data from your top five (or top ten if you're in a large market) competitors:

- website address
- days and hours of operation
- number of years in business
- ages of children served
- total capacity by age of child
- total vacancies by age of child
- child-to-teacher ratios by age of child
- registration fees
- tuition rates
- special accreditations
- unique benefits or market niche
- unique value statement (see chapter 12 for information about unique value statements)

- guarantees offered
- enrollment special offers or promotions

To gather the key information about your competitors, you have to observe your competitors. In a sense, you have to spy on them. Some of you may feel uncomfortable doing this sort of detective work—it may seem strange for people in a caring industry to be competitive—but it's important that you do it anyway. You are a business leader in the end, and all successful business leaders study their competitors.

Complete a competitive market analysis worksheet to capture all of the pertinent information you collect about each of your competitors (see figure 10-1 for an example). The information collected will help you see how your child care business fits into your market and what competitive advantage you have or should have.

Here are some of the benefits of collecting the competitive data and of analyzing your competition:

- It's the best way to determine whether your rates are too low or too high. Are you leaving money on the table?
- You will immediately know if your fees, hours, or other characteristics are out of sync with your market.
- You can study the websites and marketing materials of your competitors, from which you may gain ideas for your program.
- You'll see more clearly your unique niche in the child care market and how you can differentiate yourself from the other child care programs in town.
- It will lead to new ideas for how to innovate and create more value in your program.
- It's the best way find that sweet spot of clientele that no one is currently serving.

Now go ahead and model the format of the sample competitive analysis provided in figure 10-1 to complete your own competitive analysis. There are a few different ways to go about gathering the key information. If you're friendly with other business owners or directors in your market, consider

Figure 10-1: Sample Competitive Analysis Form

Competitive Analysis	Competitor 1	Competitor 2	Competitor 3
Longevity	opened 2001	opened 2004	opened 2006
Web address	www.schoolb.com	www.schoolc.com	www.schoold.com
Ages of children served	6 weeks to 10 years	6 weeks to 12 years	6 weeks to 12 years
Unique benefits	positioned as the "Gold Standard"	offers full elementary; international flavor; French, yoga, and music included in tuition	NAEYC accredited
Offers/promotions			
Registration fee	$100 per family	$50 per child	$70 per child
Comparative pricing (full-time)			
• infants	$275	$235	$253
• toddlers	$258	$215	$225
• preschool	$205	$195	$198
Ratios			
• infants	4:1	4:1	5:1 or 2:12
• toddlers		8:1	7:1
• preschool		12:1	10:1
Hours of operation			6:30 a.m. to 6:30 p.m. M through F
Total capacity	128	160	157
Total vacancies	30	14	62
Vacancy rate	23%	9%	39%
Strengths	brand-new state-of-the-art facility; appeals to affluent parents who want "the best"	low price for perceived value; French, Spanish, music included	huge indoor playset; large outdoor play area; NAEYC accredited; 1-Star Rating
Weaknesses	may feel too corporate; highest priced	small outdoor play area; surrounded by concrete	staff turnover; high ratios
Accreditations	independent accreditation	??	Star Rated; NAEYC accredited

simply phoning them or meeting with them yourself, talking to them directly. Be careful not to discuss rates, however, because it could be considered a violation of federal anti-trust law. (For more information about why, see "Can You Legally Discuss Your Child Care Rates?" on *Tom Copeland's Taking Care of Business* blog, http://tomcopelandblog.typepad.com.)

As another option, ask a member of your team, a friend, or an extended family member to help you by acting as a "mystery shopper." You could also hire a professional mystery shopping company to be an objective researcher. In any case, collect information over the phone and visit competitors' websites. Request information via their "contact us" link. Check into and follow along with their enrollment-building process. When you do, you will learn how skilled your competitors are at following up with prospects, and you'll see what types of promotional materials they mail to prospects. You'll find out whether your competitors continue to contact prospective customers at regular intervals after the first inquiry. Depending on what you discover, you may decide to adopt some of their techniques for your own program.

 To conduct a full and accurate competitive analysis, Tom and Juanita decided to have their daughter Caroline do some "mystery shopping" on their behalf—she contacted and visited each of their competitors' centers. Caroline is a new mom who lives in another town about forty miles away. Tom and Juanita were extremely pleased with the results of the process. Caroline brought back specific information about capacities, rates, marketing materials, areas of each tour that were impressive, and aspects of each tour that were weak. For example, she liked one program particularly well because they had a new playground that incorporated nature-based learning concepts. This feature really set them apart from the others. On the other hand, Caroline felt that all of the centers she visited were lacking somewhat in professionalism, because none of the directors shook her hand, and some of the teachers seemed distracted and frazzled during the tour. Tom and Juanita used this information to refine their tour and enrollment processes and to start communicating their unique benefits and key differences more effectively. They also adjusted their rates to be at parity with one of their core competitors. They found their conversion ratio of tours to enrollments began to improve as a result.

Finding the Unmet Need and Filling It

I've worked with child care business owners who are able to quickly fill their programs and establish their waiting lists—and who consequently are very profitable from the start—while others struggle with enrollment for months or years. Oftentimes one big thing really makes the difference: finding a segment of unmet needs in the child care marketplace and filling those needs. If there's a segment of pent-up demand in your market—perhaps for an environmentally focused program, or a program that serves organic foods, or a twenty-four-hour care program—you may be able to create a service within your program to supply that need. I have seen several child care owners determine this effectively, and they almost always fill their program to enrollment capacity very quickly, sometimes in a matter of weeks.

So how do you figure out what that unmet need is? Doing a competitive analysis to identify opportunities for adding value to your program is one good strategy. Another good strategy is simply to ask your current and potential customers whether there is something they wish was offered in area child care programs but have been unable to find. Maybe it's evening or weekend drop-in care. Maybe it's extended hours or flexible rates. Maybe it's an online video surveillance system so parents can visually connect with their children during the day, or maybe it's an outstanding indoor play space for children who live in parts of the country that have long, cold winters. It could be any number of things. The point is that acting on the unmet needs of your market—responding to the pent-up demand—might give your program the unique competitive advantage it needs to thrive.

Filling a core market need or demand is a commonsense business approach I've used with countless clients, and it works. Let me share a real-world example. A client of mine was a pediatric nurse practitioner in Brooklyn, New York. She owned her own practice, with partners, and had for many years, so she had some business experience. For a variety of reasons, she wanted to get out of the nursing profession and start something new.

She had heard over the years from many of the parents of her patients about the tremendous need for a high-quality child care program in their particular neighborhood. Indeed, parents had complained to her time after time about how they were so disheartened by the lack of a good preschool in their area. The features they requested most often were a safe and secure entrance; a full curriculum with music, dance, and Spanish; and an educated, experienced teaching staff.

Sensing a real unmet need, my client considered all of the parent feedback and took action. She left her nursing practice and created a child care program that gave the market what it was asking for. And because she listened to and responded to the market, she was able to open the new preschool at 100 percent capacity—with a waiting list of forty-eight children!

Another client of mine added organic meals to her program. No one else in her market offered organic meals; she listened to the parents and neighbors who had requested something like this in the past. Even though she had to increase her rates to cover the cost of buying organic ingredients, once she announced her new organic menu, her enrollment increased and she stayed fully enrolled for years.

The following exercise will help you take action to find the areas of pent-up demand in child care in your market. It's then up to you to fill those demands by creating the solution within your program.

Exercise 12 Find the Unmet Need(s) in Your Market

This exercise is actually an ongoing conversation between you and the important groups in your market: customers, prospects, alumni, staff, and local business partners. Make a research plan to discover what child care services or program benefits your market desires but doesn't have. Do the following:

1. Talk to existing clients. Host a focus group at your facility. Serve food as a bit of a thank-you.
2. Talk to your parent board.

3. Mail a survey to your alumni families.

4. Talk to other local child-related business owners—pediatricians, dentists, nurses, toy store owners, elementary school teachers and principals, real-estate agents.

5. Hold a brainstorming session with staff. Pick their brains about what they have seen and heard in the community.

6. Track your competitors over time and look for program changes they have made to respond to the market. If they have recently expanded or made a major shift in offerings, try to learn more about how the market is responding to them.

7. Ask the different groups questions such as these:

   • Is there some type of special service or feature you wish was offered in the area child care programs but have been unable to find?

   • What new ideas have you heard about from other parents, teachers, or staff in terms of special child care offerings or services?

   • Is there an area of town (or somewhere else) that is underserved in terms of quality child care? Could this be a profitable expansion opportunity for you?

Record feedback from these groups by keeping a binder, notebook, or computer document with all your findings. Since this is an ongoing conversation with multiple groups of people, you will want in place a handy system for referring to your notes over time.

Again, all successful business owners spend time gaining a full and complete understanding of their competitors so they can react wisely and appropriately with a clear marketing strategy that capitalizes on competitive advantages and minimizes competitive weaknesses. Even though you are in a caring profession, you must stay on top of moves in your market so your business can thrive.

Now Take Action!

We've learned a lot about the key constituencies that make up your market: current customers, past clients, prospects, competitors, community partners, and staff. Now here are some action steps you can take to apply this knowledge to your specific market that will give you tremendous insights into how to craft your marketing plan to grow your enrollment quickly and cost effectively.

- ☐ Complete the exercises right away.
- ☐ Conduct an online satisfaction survey of your parents.
- ☐ Hold a testimonial contest, and include ways for parents to provide you with audio and video testimonials.
- ☐ Create a parent communication plan.
- ☐ Create a family appreciation and loyalty-building plan, including a calendar of key dates and task due dates.
- ☐ Complete a competitive analysis of your market competition
- ☐ Contact alumni families to track the accomplishments of older children and teens who were in your program when they were younger.
- ☐ Hold informal focus groups or just talk to people in the community to find the segment(s) of unmet need in your market.

3

Message

When you discover your mission, you will feel its demand. It will fill
you with enthusiasm and a burning desire to get to work on it.
—W. CLEMENT STONE

In the land of the blind, the one-eyed man is king.
—DESIDERIUS ERASMUS

11

Crafting Your Message

So far, we've learned about how to use key business metrics to measure your business and how to really know, understand, and leverage the dynamics of your market. Now it's time to craft your message.

I've met many child care business leaders who really struggle with finding the words to dynamically convey what makes their program special, unique, and different from the other child care programs in their market. But that's what crafting your message is all about—using marketing copy to attract new families to your program and enable you (along with your staff, partners, and current customers) to accurately and effectively tell your story to others.

In the following section of the book, I will provide you with all the tools you need to effectively craft a compelling, unique, and interesting marketing message. And let me make an important point before we get started. These days, young parents are being inundated more than ever before with thousands of marketing messages—via text messages on Facebook, smartphones, and many other new media sources as well as from traditional sources, such as highway billboards and radio and television ads. The point is, if your message is boring, you have absolutely zero chance of grabbing your prospects' attention. You must work hard to craft interesting, fun, charming, even outrageous marketing messages that compel your prospects and customers to take notice of your program. The good news is that most other child care programs all look alike, sound alike, and give center tours that are incredibly similar to one another. With just a little attention to your message, you can quickly and easily stand out from the crowd and tell your unique and special story.

We will focus on three important topics as we help you craft your message:

- Unique value: You will learn what a unique value statement is and why it is critical to your success. You'll also learn about benefits compared to features and why it's important to understand the difference and be able to communicate each of them to your prospects.
- Eight key ingredients: You'll discover the eight necessary components of any compelling marketing message and how to create them. When you start incorporating these eight key ingredients into your ads, flyers, brochures, and websites, you will see a dramatic improvement in the effectiveness of your marketing.
- Effective marketing copy: You will learn some rules and guidelines for writing effective marketing copy that works to attract new families to your program. This is particularly important in today's electronic age, because parents are more likely to "pre-shop" child care choices online by reading website copy and developing an opinion about you before they even pick up the phone.

Once you gain more skills in the area of crafting your message, you will probably find yourself having a lot more fun as a marketer of your business—many of my clients tell me this is the case for them and their staff. So let's get started by handing you the tools to craft a fun, personality-filled message.

12

Finding Your Unique Value

This may sound strange, but just being good at what you do is not enough to stay fully enrolled over the long run. Lots of people in child care—lots of your competitors—are good at what they do. Your clients and prospects assume you're good at what you do because you've been professionally trained. Even the youngest, wet-behind-the-ears child care director knows more than her customers and prospects do about how to run a quality early childhood program.

Most child care business owners simply do not understand this crucial point: that simply being good at what you do is not enough. They believe that if they provide a good staff, a high-quality curriculum, and a well-maintained facility, then their phone will ring and new customers will enroll. Unfortunately, a key ingredient is missing.

And that key ingredient is uniqueness. Most child care programs suffer from sameness. They are each the clean, high-quality child care business down the street, and they haven't bothered to figure out what makes them unique or special—that is, *different* from their competitors. Moreover, most child care business owners and directors are guilty of "me-too" marketing tactics, doing themselves a disservice by presenting their program in the same manner as the child care business down the street does.

Case in point: many child care business owners take the following steps when they're getting ready to begin the enrollment process.

- Install signage at location.
- Create brochure and business cards.
- Design an ad for the local paper or Yellow Pages that looks pretty much the same as all the ads of other child care centers.

- Work hard training staff and getting accreditations.
- Open doors for business.
- Wait for the phone to ring.
- Wonder why enrollments are lower than projected.
- Scratch head and wonder what to do next!

Sound familiar? Instead of following this nonstrategic approach, you would be much smarter to craft a unique, compelling, and interesting marketing story—one that sets you apart from all the other child care programs in your town. Ideally, your website, brochure, ads, and signage would all reflect your unique identity and story. (More about this coming up.) If there's truly nothing unique, special, or different about your program compared to others in your area, you probably need to go about creating some unique features and benefits for your child care business. To use marketing jargon, what you need to do is create a *unique selling proposition*, or USP. But in the field of early childhood, I've learned that business leaders are more comfortable referring to this statement as their *unique value statement*, or UVS. A UVS answers the question, "Why should a customer choose my program instead of any other child care business in town?"

So, how do you go about creating a UVS, and how does it help you get more enrollments?

A good way to start is to identify what you believe the UVS of your competition is. You can use the competitive analysis example back in chapter 10 to figure this out by gathering your competitors' brochures and by searching their websites. And if you do the research but can't discern the benefits that make them stand out, guess what? Your competitors don't have a UVS at all! In fact, you'll find that most child care business leaders have not taken the time (or don't have the skills) to communicate or create something of unique value in their program. Moreover, most small business owners in general struggle with creating and communicating their UVS. Quite honestly, this is because finding and communicating what really makes you different can sometimes be tough to do. Let's learn more strategies about crafting your UVS to make it easier for you.

For example, say you have three key competitors in your market. Two are corporate-owned programs, and the other one, like you, is independently and locally owned by a husband-wife team. All three of the other programs are located in one section of town, and you are on the other end. So that might be one clue regarding how you are different—a unique location. Perhaps you can use something else to your advantage in your marketing message regarding location. Are you near playgrounds, parks, or other child-oriented attractions? Another thing you might notice when examining your program compared to your competitors is that your program is the only one that offers a hot lunch included with tuition, and you offer computer and arts enrichment included in tuition too. Your three competitors do not. These are all unique differences about your program that you need to focus on in your marketing message. Don't be shy about telling your prospects what is unique, different, and better about your program.

Take some time to really figure out what your competitors are doing—or not doing—to craft and communicate their UVS, as well as what makes your program unique to your market. Ask yourself what's special about your program. What do you offer parents or children that no other child care program in town can offer? If nothing stands out about your business, it's time to create something new about your program and services that will appeal to parents and children and get your community buzzing about you.

Here are some real-world examples of straightforward unique value statements that will help you craft your own.

- "Our program is the only one in town with an online video camera system parents can use to connect with their children during the day."
- "Our program has the lowest teacher-to-child ratio of any program around."
- "Our program has 'gone green,' and we offer organic meals every day!"
- "Unlike the other local programs, we teach Spanish, French, infant and toddler sign language, and piano, among other special curriculums."
- "Children enrolled in our program will be reading by their first progress report in kindergarten!"

- "We offer the largest indoor playground in town, including a faux indoor tree that kids can climb and swing from, and one that sprays water down into a water table." (Yes, they really do exist!)
- "Our program is the only one in town that offers a Jewish curriculum."

Exercise 13 Crafting Your Unique Value Statement

Fill in the answers to the following thought-jogging questions to identify possible unique qualities about your child care program compared to your competitors'.

1. What aspects or qualities of my program appear to be unique or different from most or all of my competitors?

   _____

   _____

   _____

   _____

   _____

2. What are the most common answers my clients give me when I ask, "How do you feel we are different from the other child care programs in the area?"

   _____

   _____

   _____

   _____

   _____

3. What satisfaction guarantees, promises, or company values could be brought forth to establish my UVS?

   _____

   _____

_____

_____

_____

4. What new features or services could I create in my program to differentiate us in our market and support a new UVS?

_____

_____

_____

_____

_____

Once you have your UVS defined, you will want to incorporate it into your marketing materials, such as your website, brochure, flyers, prospective parent packet, and advertisements. Your new marketing materials and plan should effectively communicate your new UVS to your target markets. We will learn more about how to choose media and create your ongoing marketing plan later in this book.

Another element of crafting your unique message is to clearly communicate features versus benefits of your child care program. Let's learn more about this now.

Features versus Benefits

Do you know the difference between a feature and a benefit? A *feature* is a characteristic of your program, such as extended hours or nutritious meals. A *benefit* is a feature communicated to the prospective customer in terms of how it's going to help them and their family to solve their problem or improve their life. And while it's fine to communicate the features of your child care program to the prospective customer, it's the benefits that are the more powerful marketing tool. When you communicate your program's benefits, prospective customers will immediately comprehend the value they will receive from your program.

The following figure illustrates a list of features and their corresponding benefits.

Figure 12-1: Features and Benefits

Feature	Benefit
A web-based video camera surveillance system	Peace of mind for parents, who can share in their child's day
Extended hours	A desire to support parents with busy schedules
Lowest teacher-to-child ratios in town	Unsurpassed individualized attention for each child
Organic meals	Kids learn to love healthy food and to make healthy food choices
Classrooms are cleaned and sanitized daily	Children's exposure to illness, germs, and bacteria is reduced

Benefits are a powerful way to communicate value. Take some time now to document and then transform your program's features into meaningful, valuable benefits for families. Think about what your customers rave about as they come and go every day. What do they rate highest about your program in customer surveys?

Exercise 14 List Your Key Features and Benefits

List your program's top ten features. Then translate each feature into a market benefit.

Feature	Benefit
1.	
2.	
3.	

4. _____ _____

5. _____ _____

6. _____ _____

7. _____ _____

8. _____ _____

9. _____ _____

10. _____ _____

Pause for a moment to review the ten benefits itemized in the exercise. Identify the benefits that are unique to your program, if any. For example, you might be the only program in your area with a special accreditation. Or perhaps your program is the only one that requires teachers to hold bachelor's degrees or higher. Even if you can't be 100 percent sure a certain benefit is unique to your program but you know it's something special (like offering baby sign language or a fully bilingual curriculum), it's a good idea to include that benefit and its corresponding feature in your marketing message.

As mentioned earlier with your UVS, once you clearly identify your unique and special benefits, be sure to include them in the message of all your promotional materials: website, ads, flyers, brochures, orientation packets, and so on. I recommend creating a page on your website titled Unique Benefits and devoting it to clearly communicating what sets your program apart from others.

In addition, make sure to train your staff on the unique benefits of your program so that your entire team is on the same page about how your program stands apart from the other centers in your area. Everyone—in particular the person responsible for answering the phone (at any hour) and conducting the tours—should rehearse their communication of program benefits so that benefits are consistently and accurately conveyed to prospects.

Consistency

Consistency in the look and the feel of your marketing materials means that your use of message elements, including marketing copy, logos, colors, images, and graphics, is the same or similar throughout all of your communication campaigns, both offline and online. The reasons for this may seem obvious: you don't want to confuse your prospect, and you do want your marketing messages to work together to complement one another.

Related to consistency is the idea of brand image or *branding*, which is the practice of promoting the name of your program and the values you want customers to associate with it. I'm often asked about branding and whether it's important for a child care business. My answer is yes and no. Let me explain.

Yes, it's important to have a consistent look and feel in your marketing materials to get the most bang out of your marketing dollars. For example, a consistent logo for your program should be used on all marketing materials, signage, and websites. Ideally you want your logo and your marketing messages to complement each other and to effectively communicate what makes your program unique and special in your market.

However, I do not recommend spending your marketing dollars on purely brand-building activities, like brand advertising or expensive logo design. *Pure brand advertising* is defined as an ad that is placed for the sole purpose of building a program's brand awareness but has no call to action. While a brand advertisement can convey qualities about your business's image or mission (often with pretty graphics and photos but without much copy), a brand ad typically does not include a call to action for the reader or viewer: no special enrollment offer, no attention-grabbing headline, and—worst of all—no unique identifier for tracking and measuring return on investment. Please don't waste your precious budget and time doing brand-advertising campaigns that you cannot track. If you can't measure an ad's effectiveness, you cannot make any fact-based decisions about whether it's working or how to improve it.

 After Tom and Juanita finished their competitive analysis and customer research, they were ready to take a hard look at how they could better tell their story. They knew they needed to spend some time gaining clarity about what makes them unique, different, and special in their market so they could craft a more powerful marketing message.

They decided to ask the advice of their chiropractor friend Mark, who originally told them about how to set up their business metrics. Mark suggested that Tom and Juanita go back to the results of their competitive analysis and take a look at the marketing materials and websites of all their competitors to learn more about how ABC Learning Center is different and unique from other programs. He also suggested they talk to their current and alumni customers to gain insights from people who actually chose them rather than other programs in the area.

Tom and Juanita implemented both of these ideas. Since they had some success with the multicultural aspect of their program and their approach to celebrating diversity, they wrote that down as a possible unique value statement as well as a unique benefit of ABC Learning Center. They made a list of all the most important features of their program and translated each into actual benefits for children and parents in their school. They created a Unique Benefits button and page on their website and added the benefits to their brochure and enrollment packet. This way they were able to gently walk prospects through the explanation of each benefit during the tour, and answer any questions the parents had about those benefits and features.

After all their implementation and research, here is what Tom and Juanita used for their unique value statement: "ABC Learning Center is the only early childhood program in the area that provides a fully accredited program in both English and Spanish. We also provide computer, music, and art enrichment programs at no extra charge to parents—everything is included in one affordable package." They incorporated their UVS into all of their marketing materials and tested different headline ideas that focused on their unique value.

Now that you've learned more about how to identify and communicate your unique value and how your program uniquely benefits local families, it's time to take your message one step further—by learning about the eight key ingredients of any effective marketing message.

13

The Eight Key Ingredients of Your Message

Child care leaders often shy away from using techniques that have been proven to work across many other industries because they feel like they shouldn't really be selling. After all, it's child care—not used cars or vacuum cleaners. So they opt to communicate gently, using a warm and fuzzy approach. It's not unusual to see a child care ad that simply lists the features of the program and nothing more. And from that, the business owner or director expects the business to come. The leads and enrollments often do not come, however, because the marketing message is not bold enough, unique enough, or compelling enough to grab the prospective customer's attention.

Marketing your business in a bold way may not be the approach recommended to you in the past. But I guarantee that if you use the techniques discussed in this chapter, your phone will ring. You simply have to take charge of your marketing message and give your prospects a compelling reason to call and then tour your facility.

Here are the eight key ingredients I recommend you include in every single piece of marketing:

- an attention-grabbing headline
- your unique value statement
- benefits
- an irresistible offer
- a deadline
- testimonials

- a guarantee or promise
- a unique identifier

I use these message elements time after time with my own company's marketing, as well as for all my child care clients—and they work! Let's dig into each one now.

Key Ingredient #1: Attention-Grabbing Headline

An attention-grabbing headline is the most important element of any marketing piece you create, whether it's a flyer, a newspaper ad, or a web page. An attention-grabbing headline is the thing that will capture a reader's attention and compel her to read your message.

Over time, cut out child care ads you find in your local media and put them in a file folder. Go to your local Yellow Pages and look at the child care ads there too. Once you've amassed a dozen or so, lay them out and review them together. Does a conspicuous pattern emerge? You'll probably notice they all look remarkably similar to one another. In fact, you could probably take one program's ad and substitute it for another's—they're that similar. Welcome to the "sea of sameness" in child care marketing. This is why it's so important for your marketing messages and ads to stand out and be different.

Here's another thing. Why do so many early childhood programs rely on the utterly meaningless headline "Now Enrolling"? Is the fact that you're now enrolling supposed to provide an irresistible benefit to the parent or to the parent's child? Why should a prospective family care? (Unless, of course, your program has a mile-long waiting list and now finally has some open slots.)

I challenge you to find something much more compelling than "Now Enrolling" for your headline! It shouldn't be too tough. You can pull several good elements into a headline to grab the reader's attention. Three of my favorite devices are curiosity, emotion, and specificity.

Curiosity

Some of the most effective headlines are set up as a question to the reader, and they evoke an intense curiosity. I'm sure you've found yourself drawn in by such a headline. Here are some examples of headlines that use the element of curiosity to engage readers:

- Why Are Parents Raving about ABC Learning Center?
- Why Are So Many Teachers and Professors Enrolling Their Children in Our Program?
- What Sets Us Apart?
- Are All Child Care Programs Equal?
- Surprising Child Care Facts for Springfield Parents: If You Have Young Children, Read This Now

Emotion

For parents, the choice of what child care program to send their child to is a very emotional one—more so than decisions related to most other service businesses. Be aware of prospective parents' emotions—their desires, needs, fears, concerns—and gently leverage them in your messaging.

Here are some examples of headlines that use the element of emotion to engage readers:

- Please Don't Take Your Most Important Investment for Granted (This headline also uses the element of curiosity.)
- All Child Care Programs Are NOT the Same
- They Laughed When My Six-Year-Old Sat Down at the Piano, but You Should Have Seen Their Faces When She Started to Play!
- The Five Secrets of Choosing Top-Quality Child Care

Specificity

People are attracted to specificity, especially if it's used in an unusual fashion. Put specific detail in your headline, such as "Get $263 of Free Child Care or a Free Gift Worth $471.27 Is Yours." Use numbers that aren't round numbers to grab attention. Here are some examples:

- An Open Letter to Springfield Residents Who Would Like $263 of Free Child Care This Month!
- Take a Center Tour and Receive a Free Gift Valued at $471.27!

Key Ingredient #2: Unique Value Statement

Whenever possible weave your unique value statement into your marketing messages. For example, if your UVS is "We are the only child care program in the area that offers second and third shift care for working parents," definitely communicate this in your marketing piece, either in the headline or the copy. Or you might even consider incorporating your UVS into the *tagline* (or slogan) accompanying your logo.

Another benefit of using your UVS in your overall marketing message is the ability to test its effectiveness. If you're not sure your UVS is as good as it could be, assess its quality by using it in an ad or mailer and measuring the number of inquiries that the piece brings to your program. Tweak the UVS, then use it in a different marketing piece, and compare its effectiveness. And so on.

Key Ingredient #3: Benefits

As discussed earlier, a feature is a characteristic of your program, like extended hours or nutritious meals. A benefit turns the feature around and restates it in the context of how it will help the customer solve their problem or improve their life. In your messaging, be sure to communicate the benefits your program can offer children and parents: bring forth your strongest benefits in the headline of your marketing piece, and use bullet points to list your benefits in the copy of the ad, flyer, brochure, or web page. Bullet points tend to be easier to read, absorb, and comprehend for the reader or viewer as compared to a lengthy paragraph of copy. Here are some examples of benefit-driven headlines that you can model for your program:

- Peace of Mind for Parents Starts Here
- We Guarantee Your Child Will Be Fully Prepared for Kindergarten
- The Best Choice You Can Make for Your Child's Future . . . and Your Family's Budget
- If Health, Wellness, and Nutrition Are Important to You, You Owe It to Yourself to Read This Message

And here is an example of program benefits in a bulleted list:

- A high level of individualized attention for your child due to our small group sizes and low teacher-to-child ratios.
- Excellent preparation for kindergarten. Our kids are well prepared for the challenges of elementary school and beyond.
- Easy access to nature, featuring regular nature walks around Hudson's ponds and picnics with the ducks!
- Conveniently located on a residential street in central Hudson, close to downtown.

Key Ingredient #4: An Irresistible Offer

This is your call to action for the reader. Your irresistible offer clearly tells the reader what you want her to do next. Give her a reason to call your program now. Make her an offer! Here are some examples of irresistible offers:

- Save Up to $350 on Child Care
- Get Two Free Weeks of Child Care PLUS Free Registration—Up to $500 Savings!
- Get Four Free Dr. Seuss Books and Four Free Weeks of Child Care When You Enroll
- Call Today to Book Your Visit and Receive a Special Set of Children's Books for Free
- Click Here for Our *Great Parenting Guide* and Receive a Complimentary Subscription to Our Newsletter

Even people who are your ideal customer are unlikely to call your business unless you actually give them a compelling reason—an offer—to do so.

Key Ingredient #5: A Deadline

Your offer, or call to action, must have a clearly stated deadline. A deadline is the best way to get people to take action; without one, they will probably put your promotion aside to come back to later—which, of course, they rarely do. Here are some examples of how to use deadlines in your marketing:

- Save Up to $350 on Child Care—Offer Expires June 30

- Enroll by June 30 and Receive Two Free Weeks of Child Care PLUS Free Registration—Up to $500 Savings!
- Get Four Free Dr. Seuss Books and Four Free Weeks of Child Care When You Enroll by Dr. Seuss's Birthday on March 2

Key Ingredient #6: Testimonials

Include at least one testimonial in every marketing piece you create—and the more, the better! You can refer to parent testimonials as "Rave Reviews" if you'd like, and you can use this theme as the primary focus of your ad. The attention-grabbing headline could read, "Why Are So Many Springfield Parents Raving About Us?" The ad copy could state your program's top unique benefits—backed up, of course, by several testimonials supporting those same benefits! Again, be sure to include the full name and city of residence of the person supplying the testimonial, which lends very important credibility. (For examples of testimonials and how to optimize their effectiveness and credibility, see chapter 9.)

Key Ingredient #7: A Guarantee or Promise

When you offer a guarantee, it automatically sets you apart from all or most of the other programs in your area. A guarantee is also a form of social proof—proof that you as the child care business owner or director are willing to put your money where your mouth is to guarantee your clients' satisfaction. I would guess that most child care programs in your area don't offer a guarantee. Why not? Because most business owners are afraid their customers might bang down their door and demand their money back. Let me assure you, this simply does not happen.

A friend of mine owns a child care center. He opened his center four years ago and has, from day one, offered the following guarantee:

Our Guarantee: We believe you and your child will love our program so much that we're willing to guarantee it. If after you enroll you become dissatisfied with our service for any reason, we will refund up to one week's tuition, no questions asked. Try us for a free day with no financial obligation. See what a difference our program will make for your child!

This friend shared with me that he has never had a single parent ask for her money back. (Of course, he has a high-quality early childhood program with top-notch teachers. If you don't feel confident enough to guarantee the quality of your program, then figure out what improvements you can make to help you feel more comfortable and secure.)

If you don't like the word "guarantee," you can offer a promise. Here is an example of how one of my clients phrases their promise:

- We promise to partner with your family in the highest goals for your child's education.
- We promise your family that we will be outstanding role models for your child and create in your child respect for authority and the value of good citizenship.

A guarantee or promise shows your prospect you are willing to stand behind the benefits and features your program offers, and it takes the risk out of their decision to do business with you. Think about your own buying decisions—don't you feel more comfortable when businesses offer you a satisfaction guarantee?

Key Ingredient #8: A Unique Identifier

Earlier in this book, we learned about why it's important for you to track your marketing return on investment as accurately as possible. One of the best ways to precisely measure your marketing ROI is to include a unique and distinct offer or offer code on each marketing piece. This means your Valpak coupon would have its very own offer code, as would your website, your brochure, each print ad, and each community event where you have a booth. So the final key ingredient for your marketing piece is this unique tracking identifier or code that will enable you to definitively measure the number of inquiries (leads) and the number of resulting enrollments you receive from each marketing effort.

Without this information, you will have no clue about which marketing pieces are working for you and which ones are not.

Figure 13-1 illustrates an example of an ad with all eight key ingredients included. Of course, if you are running small-sized ads, you may need to omit a couple of the ingredients, and that's okay. You can test different ads over time and see which ingredients work the best to bring inquiries in your market.

Figure 13-1: An Ad Containing All Eight Key Ingredients

Now use the following exercise to craft an ad, flyer, or mailer that includes all eight key ingredients.

Exercise 15 Create an Effective Marketing Piece

Complete this exercise using the eight key ingredients to create an effective marketing piece.

1. Ideas for attention-grabbing headlines (Key Ingredient #1): _____

   _____

   _____

   _____

2. Your unique value statement (Key Ingredient #2): _____

   _____

   _____

   _____

3. Key benefits of your program (Key Ingredient #3): _____

   _____

   _____

   _____

4. Irresistible offers (Key Ingredient #4) with deadlines for taking action (Key Ingredient #5): _____

   _____

   _____

   _____

5. Your strongest testimonials (Key Ingredient #6): _____

   _____

   _____

   _____

6. Your guarantee or promise (Key Ingredient #7): _____

_____

_____

_____

7. Unique identifier or offer code (Key Ingredient #8): _____

_____

_____

Refer to this exercise when creating your marketing pieces to make sure you don't forget any of the eight key ingredients.

Ever since Tom and Juanita opened their program, their marketing materials looked pretty much the same as those of all the other child care centers and preschools in their market. They worried that it would be unprofessional to adopt some of the clever and bold marketing styles they had seen other businesses use. But they knew they needed a different approach to survive in the tough economy. They noticed that one competitor in their market was making dramatic money-saving offers and using lots of unusual marketing techniques, like a satisfaction guarantee, and they heard from a reliable source that this program was nearly fully enrolled. Tom and Juanita decided to model the competitor's approach and came up with their own unique take on it. We'll learn more about their new marketing ideas in the next chapter.

By using the eight key ingredients discussed in this chapter, not only will your marketing message become much more effective, but you will have fun during the creation process! Many leaders I work with really dread the work of coming up with new marketing messages, but once they learn this approach and start applying the template of these eight ingredients to their ads, flyers, mailers, and web pages, they gain a new excitement and energy toward enrollment-building activities.

14

How to Write Effective Marketing Copy

One of the best skills you can develop—one that will truly pay off in terms of bringing you new enrollments—is learning to write effective marketing copy. Because many early childhood professionals haven't been trained in marketing techniques, their *marketing copy*—the words they use in their ads, flyers, brochures, and web pages—is often boring, ho-hum, and ineffective at attracting new families to their center or school. A good first step toward writing effective marketing copy yourself is to look at the types of ads and copy your competitors are producing—and then produce exactly the opposite! Let's learn more about how to make your copy stand out from the crowd and give you more bang for your marketing dollars.

Long Copy

Many business owners shy away from long marketing copy because they believe no one will take the time to read it. I have found this to be untrue, and here's why.

The biggest reason a qualified prospect chooses not to engage with a particular business (that is, to buy stuff from it) is a lack of trust. More than ever, consumers are wary and skeptical of marketing messages. But if through your copy you can gain the reader's trust, you've achieved a huge goal, one that most other businesses have not. So what's the best way to gain that trust? Social proof, testimonials, word of mouth, and satisfaction guarantees are great techniques. Two more are to *tell your story* and to *communicate benefits* to the reader.

Oftentimes, to include all those trust-building techniques in your copy, your copy needs to be long.

Most ads, especially those for early childhood programs, don't do enough to sell the prospect. An ad should tell the reader everything she needs to know about your child care service to equip her with the information she needs to make a buying decision. It should tell her who you are and why she should care, why your service is unique, and why the purchase decision is free of risk. Of course not everyone is going to read all of that copy! But the people who are your best prospects will. Your best prospects are shopping for child care right now, and your ad, with its copy longer than most, will begin to build trust and forge a relationship with them at the moment they start reading it.

Include Bullet Points

Incorporate bullet points into your copy—they make copy easy to read. People are more likely to read a list of well-written points than lots of long paragraphs, especially in *digital marketing* copy, such as on websites, in banner ads online, and in your e-mail blast messages to prospects and customers.

Here is a before-and-after example of an e-mail blast one of my clients planned to send to prospects and customers. In figure 14-1, because the text is presented without bullet points, you as the reader are less likely to absorb the main points of what the e-mail is trying to convey. With the addition of bullet points in figure 14-2, the copy "pops" more to the reader's eye and is easier to read.

Figure 14-1: An Ad without Bullet Point Copy

Edu-Camp
Summer 2011 @ ABC

ABC Learning Center is announcing
Edu-Camp for children ages two through nine!
This summer will be dedicated to

discovering what we want to be when we grow up!

Children ages two through five will enjoy weekly in-house entertainment, demonstrations and shows, physical education with Mr. Pearson, walking field trips, and water days at ABC!

The newly created program for older children ages six through nine will include the same great experiences plus swimming at East Woods and trips to Colony Park for physical education with Mr. Pearson!

Figure 14-2: An Ad with Bullet Point Copy

"Mommy, when I grow up I want to be…"

This summer at ABC Learning Center, children ages two through nine will be immersed in **discovering what they want to be when they grow up!** Your child will have a blast and learn so much.

Children ages 2–5 will enjoy:

- exciting weekly themes
- demonstrations and shows
- games with Coach Pearson
- walking field trips
- water days at ABC

Children ages 6–9 will enjoy:

- weekly activities and themes
- demonstrations and shows
- sports with Coach Pearson
- field trips to the parks and science center
- swimming at East Woods pool

"Enrolling our children at ABC is one of the best decisions we've ever made."
—Tom and Kim Field (parents of Ethan, Emily, and Sam)

Check out our weekly schedule of events!

Tell Your Story

As children, most of us were raised to love stories, and we are naturally drawn in by the words "Let me tell you a story." One great technique for engaging the reader with your marketing copy is to *tell your story*—who you are and why the reader should care. For example, you might tell the story of how and why you came to be a child care business owner or director; the story of your own children, grandchildren, or neighborhood children who attended your program; or a story about one of your teachers who won an excellence award. Stories draw people to you, and as they get to know you better, they will begin to like and trust you.

The Know-Like-Trust Principle

Across any type of business, the *know-like-trust principle* holds true: people do business with people they know, like, and trust. Your promotional offer, attention-grabbing headline, or satisfaction guarantee may be what gets that prospective parent to call you, but it's not going to keep her with you or cause her to refer friends and coworkers to your program. At the end of the day, your customers do business with you because they know you, they like you, and above all else, they entrust you with their most precious gift—their children.

If your marketing messages can build trust and rapport and credibly convey the reasons people should trust you (circling back again to the absolute need for social proof—client testimonials and positive word of mouth), you will gain and retain customers.

The Problem-Agitate-Solve Copywriting Technique

The *problem-agitate-solve copywriting technique* has been around for a long time and has been used with great success in many industries and types of businesses. The general idea of this technique is to present a *problem* that your prospect will identify with, to *agitate* that problem by making the prospect realize how bad it is or could get, and then to demonstrate how your product or service can *solve* the problem.

The following direct mail letter illustrates the problem-agitate-solve copy-writing technique used to promote a child care program.

Figure 14-3: A Direct Mail Letter Illustrating Problem-Agitate-Solve

Entering the Conversation Already Occurring in the Minds of Your Prospects and Customers

This copywriting technique, popularized by leading copywriter and marketer Dan Kennedy, is very powerful. Using this technique, you write copy that ties your marketing message into what people in your market are already talking about and thinking about: current news events, celebrity gossip, hit TV shows, upcoming holidays, news-making weather patterns, or seasonal changes. Another great one is holidays. Entering the conversation about an upcoming holiday—tying your ads, flyers, mailers, and even signage to Valentine's Day, Mother's Day, the Fourth of July, St. Patrick's Day, or Thanksgiving—can be particularly effective, because holidays have universal appeal; people are already chatting about them by the water cooler. Using this copywriting technique is sure to get your marketing messages noticed, and you can have a lot of fun getting creative with it.

Exercise 16 Develop Your Copywriting Skills

Answer the following questions. Use the answers for ideas and inspiration to improve your copywriting efforts.

1. Tell your story of how and why you started this child care business, or why you wanted to work in early childhood. What makes your story special, poignant, and interesting?

\
\
\
\
\
\

2. Do you have any fun, interesting, even wacky stories about things that have happened in your program? For example, a teacher who dressed up as a leprechaun and painted himself green on St. Patrick's Day? Use any charming, interesting, and heartwarming stories.

\
\
\
\
\
\
\

3. What is happening in current events that you might be able to leverage in your marketing copy? Here's an idea: "Did you know that the creators of Google were Montessori students?"

_____

_____

_____

_____

_____

_____

4. What holidays can you plan to tie into with your marketing offers and copy? What holidays do you currently celebrate that you can extend to your marketing or use to attract the community?

_____

_____

_____

_____

_____

_____

Tom and Juanita noticed that their friend Mark used the story of his two big dogs in his marketing—the dogs became the mascots of Mark's chiropractic business. The dogs modeled the fun, interesting, and wacky marketing copy he used to attract clients—after all, his ads were getting a reputation in the community for being unique, different, fresh, and best of all fun to read! Tom and Juanita realized that even though they offered a high-quality program and wanted their customers to take them seriously as professionals, they could still be a little outrageous in marketing to attract the attention of new prospects, to give them a reason to get to know them better. Tom came up with the idea of tying in with Cinco de Mayo because it is a fun holiday that all of the families in his program could relate to. Juanita took a photo of Tom wearing her father's traditional Mexican clothing, including a sombrero and maracas, and they used the photo to promote their program's Cinco de Mayo fiesta for families, along with a special enrollment offer. The promotion was advertised in the local paper, via e-mail to their list, on their signage, and in a direct mail postcard campaign. The campaign created some buzz among friends, families, and prospects in the community—and resulted in the enrollment of five new children. Juanita and Tom started planning more marketing campaigns like this for the remainder of the year.

One of the best skills you can develop as the marketer of your child care program is learning to write effective marketing copy. Become a student of good copy by constantly looking at different media. Clip ads that appeal to you through their use of story, personality, problem-agitate-solve, by tying into holidays, or by entering the conversation going on in your mind. Start noticing how these ads are more effective at grabbing your attention and allowing you to begin liking and trusting the business that ran the ad.

Now Take Action!

Your marketing messages are critical to getting your phone to ring and convincing people to take time out of their day to visit your program. The strategies and techniques presented in part 3 of this book have been used successfully by many different types of small businesses, including early childhood businesses. Get your program out of the "sea of sameness" and make your marketing message unique, interesting, fun, charming, or just plain different.

Apply the strategies and techniques recommended in the preceding chapters. Your phone will start ringing almost overnight when you take these action steps.

- ☐ Complete the exercises right away.
- ☐ Pull out all the messaging you are currently using in your enrollment packet for prospects, brochures, Yellow Pages, web pages, flyers, and ads. Do a comprehensive audit of all your marketing messages. Make notes, add sticky notes, edit your materials, or do whatever method you prefer to incorporate the eight key ingredients you have learned about.
- ☐ Gain the trust of your prospects by using social proof, testimonials, success stories, and a money-back satisfaction guarantee. Make sure your materials and website communicate the benefits of your program to the reader.
- ☐ Create a holiday promotion calendar, which will provide you with a framework for planning your holiday promotions.

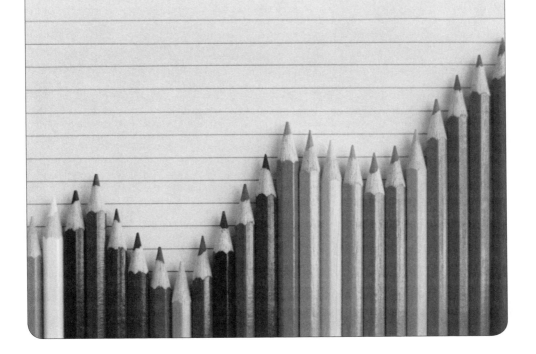

PART

4

Media

If you can find a path with no obstacles,
it probably doesn't lead anywhere.
—FRANK A. CLARK

15

Choose and Use Media Effectively

Now it's time to learn more about the fourth and final pillar of effective child care marketing: media. *Media* are the methods you will use, such as magazines, direct mailers, community events, and online marketing, to reach your target market. If you've been implementing the action steps provided in this book, you've by now accumulated more knowledge about child care marketing and what works to build enrollment than most child care leaders. You should have a higher degree of clarity about your metrics, your market, and your message. You have done research on your ideal target market, both demographically and geographically. You have completed your competitive analysis and identified some community businesses to partner with. You have in essence discovered your voice—the core elements of your marketing message. Now it's time to choose what media you're going to use to reach your target market with your message.

Based on my experience working to grow the enrollment of early childhood businesses, you should consider six important media choices for your marketing plan:

Online media—your website. Information about your child care program on the Internet that can be easily found by young parents in your market and can do a good job of communicating what you have to offer.

Online media—social media. Websites where people gather online to communicate, bond, share photos, and get to know others like them can be great for your business. Facebook and Twitter are two of the most popular social media sites right now.

Community marketing. Any media used to reach out to local residents and business partners, such as local events and cross-promotional campaigns with other businesses is community marketing.

Publicity campaigns. Using press releases and developing relationships with local media representatives is a great way to promote your business.

Direct mail. Any messages you send directly to the home address of your customers or prospects, such as letters, greeting cards, postcards, or thank-you notes are direct mail.

Local media advertising. Ads placed in your town's newspaper or a regional magazine, or on a local radio station or television station are local media advertising.

This is not a complete list of all the media choices you should consider, but if your marketing plan uses all or most of these, you will be well on your way to expanding awareness of your program and increasing the number of leads you receive.

Now you may wonder, "What about word of mouth? Where does that fit in?" Great questions. Word of mouth is indeed the most powerful form of advertising, but it's not a true type of media—it's the result of using all the techniques we've been learning about in this book. When you implement exceptional customer service, fun and unique marketing messages, and an overall high level of value to your customers, you will indeed generate more word of mouth in your community. Throughout this section we'll learn more ideas about how media choices impact word of mouth and the buzz your program generates.

One important aspect of an effective marketing plan is to be able to measure each marketing effort so you can reliably estimate how many leads—and then enrollments—that effort brings. We discussed how to track your marketing return on investment metrics back in chapter 4, so if you need a refresher on how to measure and track each effort, you may want to revisit that chapter. In any case, you will likely find that certain media work better than others, and that's to be expected.

The chapters that follow cover in detail the six media choices named above. When you understand the dos and don'ts of each media form, you will be better able to choose and effectively use each of them. The last chapter in this part of the book tells you how to set your marketing budget—that is, how much you should allocate overall, and how to test and make adjustments to your plan over time. Now let's go deeper.

16

Online Media: Your Website

Over the last few years, there's been a huge shift—a veritable sea change—in the way parents of young children obtain information about child care programs in their area. According to an independent study cited by eMarketer .com ("Local Searchers Head to Store More," October 23, 2009), people looking for child care use specialized local search engines. Clearly your program's online presence—your website, specifically—is crucial to building enrollment. After all, if the goal of your effective marketing plan is to get fully enrolled by reaching the right customers with the right message using the right media, not only must you have a website for your program, but you absolutely must work to optimize it to communicate your unique message and stand out from the competition. I can honestly tell you that the vast majority of my clients experience huge gains in inquiries and enrollments when they optimize their website message and make sure it's ranking high on the search engines.

In this chapter, you will learn about the major advantages of websites compared to other forms of media, how to optimize your website's performance, how to keep it updated and maintained, how to generate targeted traffic to your site, and how to use e-mail marketing in conjunction with it.

First, let's learn more about the advantages of using websites and e-mail as compared to other media. There are four big benefits to using these online media:

Low cost. Online media are typically inexpensive compared to traditional media. You can create a nice website for less than $2,000—sometimes for even less than $1,000—and pay just a few dollars a month to have it hosted. E-mail is, for now, free. Taken together, a website and e-mail can help you generate new prospects and communicate with them for just pennies per lead.

Speed. Online media are very fast. To communicate quickly with your audience, you simply can't come by anything faster. For example, if you have to communicate an emergency situation to your parents, an instant e-mail broadcast will get the message out much faster than phone calls or notes. It can save you and your staff tons of time.

A growing audience. Every hour millions of people use the Internet to get information and make purchase decisions, and the numbers are growing every day. People from all walks of life and every country on the planet use the Internet; even seniors are going there in droves. Children are tuned in, too; when they grow up they will undoubtedly be online even more than their parents' generation. And with the ever-growing use of smart phones and web applications, people are spending more time online than ever.

It's easy to change and test. Compared to a printed brochure, it's much easier, faster, and cheaper to make changes to your website and other online marketing pieces, such as promotional offers, headlines, testimonials, images, and your logo. That means you can better afford to test the effectiveness of your marketing messages online compared to traditional offline media. For example, Timothy Ferriss, author of the bestseller *The 4-Hour Workweek*, used Adwords, Google's pay-per-click program, to test different ideas for the title of his book. He didn't actually like the title *The 4-Hour Workweek*, but it was overwhelmingly the most popular one—that is, the one that got the most clicks—when he tested it online. Things you can test with your online pages include different headlines, enrollment offers, benefit and feature copy, and different types of satisfaction guarantees or promises.

Online media are not, however, perfect. One of the big challenges is to get and keep the attention of your prospects and customers. People move quickly around on the web. You literally have about two seconds to make a good impression and draw the prospect into your website. This is why it is incredibly important for you to use an attention-grabbing headline, some compelling images (photos of kids in your program are always great), and bullet point copy that's easy to read and digest.

Maximize Your Website Success in Three Steps

If you want to become and stay fully enrolled, your child care program simply must have a website, preferably one that's optimized for local search results. Let's learn more about how you can maximize the success of your website in three easy steps: create, automate, populate.

Step 1: Create

You need a well-designed website that clearly communicates your message—it needs to convey to the prospect the qualities of your program that make it unique in your market, that set it apart from your competitors. Your website needs to do an excellent job of promoting your program so it can act as a lead-generating machine. The number one responsibility of your website is to bring new leads to your program.

One way to create a well-designed website is to hire a web marketing company to do it for you. An advantage of using a local website development company rather than a large national company is that it has ties to your community and may respond faster to your needs in order to get a great referral from you. And you can have face-to-face meetings, which sometimes make communication clearer than by phone or e-mail. A good way to find a solid, reputable website development company in your area is to ask colleagues and other local business owners, ones you trust and whose websites you like, for recommendations.

Another way is to simply create the website yourself, or ask a staff member or a parent from your program to create it. While this route is much less expensive than hiring a website development company, I recommend it only if you have solid technology skills—knowledge of HTML, for example, the language used to create websites.

Blogs

If you don't know HTML but want to do the work of creating your own website, consider a blog-based website. It's quick and fairly easy to create a blog-based website, and once you have, it's quick and fairly easy to make updates and upload photos and video. And a blog integrates well with social networking sites like Facebook, because comments that people post on your blog can be fed directly to your Facebook page and other social media sites. For more information on how to set up a blog, get a book such as *WordPress for Dummies* (2010, Wiley Publishing), which walks you through the process.

No matter what route you take to create your website, begin the process by surfing the web and finding sites that appeal to you. These can be child care websites or others. Analyze their design, layout, and copy. Are the graphics pleasing? Is the site easy to navigate? Is the contact information clear on every page? Take note of the sites you like. Write down their URLs or bookmark them. When it's time to work with your website team, refer to these examples to give them an idea of what you like and how to create your site navigation and design.

Design

Here are what I consider to be five must-have website-design elements:

Appealing presentation. You want your website to be visually uncluttered and attractive. Use happy colors and images that convey the unique personality of your program, but keep it simple and easy on the visitor's eyes.

Interesting but simple copy. Include a compelling headline, one that grabs the reader's attention, followed by a clearly stated unique value statement and your program's core benefits, preferably in a bulleted list.

Well-planned, simple navigation. Your website should be easy to navigate, and your contact information—your phone number and street address—should be easy to find on every page. Be sure to include main navigation buttons to important content pages, such as parent and staff testimonials ("Rave Reviews"), your unique benefits ("What Makes Us Special"), frequently asked questions ("FAQs"), and the history of your program ("Our Story").

A call to action. Now that prospects have found your site, what should they do next? Be sure to include a way for customers to request more information online by entering their name and e-mail address.

Multimedia (video and audio). Your home page should feature a brief video visitors can watch to get a sense of what your child care program is all about. Use a small flip camera or another handheld video camera to take some footage of your child care program in action, or have a video created by a professional. Either way, you can post the video to YouTube and easily link it to your site. Audio can help make your site come alive too. Record an audio welcome message, or have customers record audio testimonials and highlight them on your site.

Maintenance

Keep in mind as you create your website that it will have to be maintained and updated. Are you going to pay a professional team to do this, or will you have a technically savvy staff member manage it all? Be sure to have a plan in place with your website creation team—ideally one that provides for updates and maintenance to be easy, fast, and inexpensive over time. Nothing is more frustrating than wanting to make changes to your website and having a slow, unresponsive, or broken process for doing so.

 ABC Learning Center had a website, but it was very dated; Tom and Juanita had not made any major updates to it since creating it back in 2002. They attended a silent auction in their community where Juanita bid on creation of a new website from a website company they were familiar with. They were the winning bidder and purchased their new website for $980, which was a pretty good bargain compared to the stated retail value of $1,750. Their designer told them to first spend some time researching the Internet, looking for child care websites they really liked and wanted to model. They did so, and found a couple of designs that really appealed to them. From there it took about two months to get their new website built and functioning. The site had a top navigation with buttons called "Our Story," "Testimonials," "Unique Benefits," "Programs," "FAQ," and "Contact Us."

Step 2: Automate

Once you've created your website, the next step is to automate its lead generation. When you do, it will become a lead generation machine, one that sends great prospects your way and brings lots of new enrollments! One of the best ways to automate your website is by using an e-mail management system to build a list of prospects, and then develop a relationship with them over time using e-mail. A side benefit of using an e-mail management system is its very low cost—often just $20 per month or so—which will enable you to communicate cost effectively with new prospects for just pennies per lead.

So what is an *e-mail management system*? It's an online software application that allows you to gather leads and store them in an online database, accessed only by you through your account. Typically you sign up as a customer with an e-mail management service, like Constant Contact (see sidebar for more information), and your account is automatically charged a low monthly (or annual) fee to use the service. This is the system you would use to communicate with all your target audiences via e-mail—you could create unique and separate lists for customers, prospects, alumni, business partners, even staff. If you have multiple school locations, you can set up your e-mail service to have unique lists based on location. Core functions of any e-mail management system include opt-in forms for gathering leads, autoresponder e-mails, and broadcast e-mail capability. Let's learn more about each.

> **TIP:** There are many e-mail management systems to choose from. I recommend three: Constant Contact (www.constantcontact.com), AWeber (www.aweber.com), and iContact (www.icontact.com). Each is very affordable—around $18 to $25 per month—and most have a free trial so you can test each one to see which suits you best before you commit.

Opt-In Forms

Have you ever visited a website and entered your name and e-mail address to receive more information or a free gift? That's an example of an *opt-in form*. You opt in when you provide your name, e-mail address, and perhaps your U.S. postal mailing address to receive something of value to you.

Opt-in forms have several advantages. First, they allow you to start building a database of interested prospects—parents and others who want to be on your mailing list to get to know more about your child care program. The opt-in form helps you gather the names and e-mail addresses of your interested prospects, which is the first step in using online marketing to build relationships. When prospects provide this information, they give you permission to start communicating with them. On your opt-in form, you can also include fields for the prospect's postal mailing address and phone number to communicate with them offline. And if you gather their postal mailing addresses, you can map them out to get a better idea of where the prospects are geographically located. This is a very smart marketing strategy. You leave money on the table when you don't do it.

Exercise 17 Opt In to Other Child Care Websites

Complete the steps in this exercise for insight into your competitors' e-mail marketing campaigns and for ideas you can model or adopt in your own program.

1. When doing your competitive research, see whether any of your competitors' sites offer an opt-in form. If they do, join their list(s).
2. Read what they send you and pay attention to any promotions, special offers, or free gifts. What do you see that you might model for your own program?
3. Consider opting in to other non–child care businesses too. If you get a great series of e-mail communications and promotions from the local children's clothing store, toy store, or salon, can you adapt them for your program?

Autoresponders

When someone opts in to your mailing list, their contact information is added to your database, and you can then start sending them e-mail communications using either an autoresponder or a broadcast e-mail. First, let's learn about *autoresponders*—simple computer programs that automatically send out marketing and relationship-building e-mail messages that you or a member of your team can write in advance. After you write them, the messages are stored in the e-mail management system as an autoresponder series, along with information you provide the system about when to send the messages out.

 Tom and Juanita were advised by their website consultant to integrate an e-mail management system into the functionality of their website so they could build a list of prospects to develop relationships with via e-mail. Here is the series of e-mails initially set up by Tom and Juanita in the e-mail management system for ABC Learning Center. They set up these messages to go out automatically on the first, second, and fourth days after their prospect opts in to receive more information about ABC Learning Center.

E-mail #1: Sent on Day 1

Title: Firstname, Attached Is the ABC Learning Center Info Packet You Requested

Dear Firstname,

Thank you for inquiring about ABC Learning Center. We are a family-owned, independent child care business, and we're proud to be the longest-running preschool in the area, with over fifteen years of experience. Our philosophy is based on highly trained and experienced teachers providing excellent curriculum in a loving environment that feels like home. Attached is the info packet you requested from our website. We are proud of the many rave reviews we've received from moms and dads just like you. ;-)

Searching for your child's learning "home" can be a difficult and emotional process. We hope that the information we provide over the next few days may make that process easier so you can find the perfect solution to your child care needs—whether it's our program or someone else's.

Briefly, here's what makes ABC Learning Center unique:

- Bilingual learning throughout the program: all teachers are fully bilingual in English and Spanish
- Our 100% Smiles Satisfaction Promise

- Low child-teacher ratios and small class sizes (deemed highly important to child care quality by the National Association of Childcare Resource and Referral Agencies)
- Nationally accredited by NECPA

When you are ready to meet our friendly, professional staff and see how much fun the little ones are having at our school, give us a call at 888-555-1212 to book a tour. We will welcome you and your child any time, as we have an "open door" policy—or if you'd like to drop by any time, that's fine too.

We look forward to meeting you and your child!

Warm regards,
Juanita and Tom, Owners

E-mail #2: Sent on Day 2

Title: Firstname, Why Is Accreditation Important for a Child Care Program?

Hi, Firstname,

Yesterday we sent you our info packet, and we hope you've had time to review it. As you gather information about child care, you may have more questions, and that's why we're here. Please do not hesitate to contact us with any questions or concerns as you make your child care or preschool choice.

In the meantime, we thought you might be interested in learning a little more about early childhood accreditation programs and why they make a difference for parents. Becoming an accredited school and maintaining the level of quality accreditation required is no easy accomplishment and should not be taken lightly. It means we hold ourselves to high standards. And we're dedicated to maintaining those standards consistently throughout our school.

ABC Learning Center holds a national accreditation from NECPA, which stands for National Early Childhood Program Accreditation. NECPA assesses quality in the areas of adult and child interaction, staff framing, health and safety, physical environment, administration, and parent and community relationships. A strong emphasis has been placed on current developments in health and safety, brain research, and risk management. The NECPA Commission is dedicated to promoting high-quality early childhood programs across the country and internationally.

When you're researching and considering different child care programs, ask about accreditation, and make note of which programs are and are not accredited. We're proud of the work we've done and continue to do in this area—because it makes a difference in the quality of care our area children receive.

We look forward to meeting you and your child!

Warm regards,
Juanita and Tom, Owners

P.S. To read more rave reviews and watch some video testimonials, please visit <our website>.

E-mail #3: Sent on Day 4

Title: Firstname—Important Questions to Consider When Choosing Child Care

Hi, Firstname,

We know that choosing the right early learning program for your child can be difficult. That's why we're writing today. After more than fifteen years of serving the child care needs of Springfield mommies and daddies just like you, we know a thing or two about educating and protecting little ones. Other moms and dads have told us this simple list of questions was helpful to them—and we hope you find it useful too.

Ten Questions to Consider When Choosing Child Care:

1. History/longevity: How long has the program been in business in this community?
2. Ratios: What are the ratios of teachers to children in each room? Are children getting enough individual attention?
3. Class sizes: How many children are in the classroom? Studies show that small class sizes are better learning environments for young children.
4. Food preparation: Does the program have a full commercial kitchen to prepare home-cooked meals? How often are fresh fruits and vegetables versus canned or frozen ones served?
5. Accreditation: What accreditations, if any, does the program hold? How often is the accreditation renewed?

6. Curriculum: Does the program use a standard curriculum, or does it create its own? How long has it used the particular curriculum, and why does it feel the curriculum provides the best education to students?

7. Cleanliness: How clean are the bathrooms, floors, surfaces, and kitchen? Is food sealed? What are the program's policies and procedures for sanitizing toys? Ask to see records.

8. Space/change of environment: Does the school have separate rooms for various daily activities and specials, or will your child remain in his same classroom all day without a change of scenery?

9. Sincerity of staff: Do the teachers and staff seem passionate about working there, and do they love what they do? Is caring for the children a calling, or is it just a j-o-b? Listen to your gut.

10. Security: Does the facility have secure doors and safety gates in good condition? Can you observe your child via video monitor, either online or in the director's office? Are entry and exit points controlled?

We look forward to meeting you and your child!

Warm regards,
Juanita and Tom, Owners

P.S. To read more rave reviews and watch some video testimonials, please visit <our website>.

As you can see, using a series of e-mail follow-ups set up in advance via autoresponder dramatically reduces the amount of time you need to spend sending prospects basic information about your program. It's a great way to put your prospect relationship-building on autopilot and eliminate the task of manually keeping track of e-mails you've sent or need to send to potential customers. Your prospects will be able to unsubscribe whenever they choose and can do so automatically using the Unsubscribe feature of your chosen e-mail management system. Thus, you will have a constantly fresh database of the names and e-mail addresses of prospects and clients.

Broadcast E-mail

Another primary function of e-mail management systems is *broadcast e-mail,* sometimes referred to as an e-mail blast. Now that you've begun building a database of prospects who have opted in to receive information via e-mail, you can use a broadcast e-mail to reach them all at once. In a broadcast e-mail you can send your prospects newsworthy information, such as an upcoming enrollment special or promotion, a special community or charitable event your program is participating in, and other entertaining updates—even your monthly e-newsletter.

Again, because of the low cost, speed, and ease, e-mail management systems are a fantastic tool for easily staying in front of your prospects and customers and keeping your program top-of-mind with your customers and prospects. These systems will help you run your online website media in a cost efficient and effective manner.

In general, most marketing experts agree that it takes seven or more contacts with a potential customer to convince them to become a buyer. Just because a prospect says no or "Let me think about it" the first time you try to get them to enroll certainly does not mean that they will never enroll. If you use e-mail marketing as a part of your online website media to follow up with your prospects in fun, entertaining, and educational ways over time, they may very well decide to enroll with you—even a year or more after they first visited your program. And if they feel they know, like, and trust you, they will be very likely to forward your e-mails to friends, neighbors, or coworkers who are seeking quality child care.

Step 3: Populate

Now that your program's well-designed website is created and you have the ability to communicate with prospects automatically, it's time to populate your site—that is, to drive traffic to your site. You can use various methods to do this. Some are free, and some you have to pay for. Let's discuss both types in more detail.

Free Traffic Sources

I recommend you start populating your website by using as many free or low-cost traffic strategies as possible. When you spend some time learning about free traffic-generating strategies, you'll become more web savvy, which will help you feel more confident about the sometimes-confusing world of paid online media.

You can drive free traffic to your website in many different ways, such as the following:

- inbound links
- search engine optimization (SEO)
- free online directories
- article marketing

Keep in mind the distinction between traffic and targeted traffic: *traffic* is the total number of unique visitors who come to your website for a given time frame, while *targeted traffic* is the total number of your ideal prospects who come there. While some free traffic sources can generate a great volume of visitors to your website, if the people who land there are not your ideal target market, then that free traffic source is not as valuable as, for example, one that sends you only affluent young parents from your best neighborhood. Ideally your free traffic sources will be targeted to reach not only parents of young children in your market, but also parents of young children who are the best fit with what your program offers in your market. Because each of the following traffic-generating tactics takes some time to implement, focus on those that will give you the highest level of targeted traffic. Let's learn about each strategy in more detail:

Inbound links. Inbound links are one of the best methods you can use to drive traffic to your website. Plus they're a top tactic for optimizing your website to rank well in the local search results. An *inbound link* exists when another website links to your site—for example, you are a member of your local Chamber of Commerce, and the chamber's site links to your site. In general, the more inbound links you have from other sites, the higher you will rank on Google, Yahoo!, and the other search engines. Inbound links are one of the top methods the search engines use to determine the relevance and legitimacy of your company's website across the entire World Wide Web. Both quantity (number of inbound links) and quality (the relevance of sites who link to you) are important.

How do you get inbound links? One way is to make a list of community partners and organizations you're a member of and investigate whether they make a practice of linking to other businesses in their organization or group. If they do, ask them to link to your program's home page. For example, if you're a member of the local Chamber of Commerce, your state child care association, and the Rotary Club, you should be able to get inbound links to your site from each of those groups' websites fairly easily. Always offer to post a link on your site to theirs in exchange, which will create a reciprocal relationship: they drive traffic to your site, and you drive traffic to theirs. The more inbound links you have, the higher you will rank on the search engines in general. You simply cannot have too many inbound links to your website.

Search engine optimization (SEO). When someone is doing an Internet search for child care in your town or ZIP code area, it's important that your business be among those at the top of the search results. To ensure this, you need to use *search engine optimization (SEO)*, that is, optimize your website to capture your top search phrases or keywords. *Keywords* are the most common words and phrases your prospects use to find your service or product when searching the Internet. For example, if your program is located in Boise, Idaho, here are some keyword phrases your website should be optimized for:

- child care Boise
- child care centers in Boise, ID
- day care Boise Idaho
- preschools in Boise
- Boise ID day care centers

As you can see, parents may use many different combinations of terms to find child care in their area. Take some time to track where your program comes up among various search results using different keyword phrases, and make it your goal to continuously improve your site's ranking on each of the major search engines. To do this, you need to optimize your website.

You can learn to optimize your website yourself, or you can hire an SEO expert to do it for you. An SEO expert can optimize your website by making changes to the text and layout of your pages, as well as by adding inbound links from other sites and directories.

It takes about three to four hours to optimize each individual page within your website, which consists of inserting the meta tags for your program's best keywords into your site's HTML source code and adding some keyword phrases to the copy on each page. Ongoing link-building campaigns are important, too, and should be managed by a skilled individual on your staff (or by your SEO expert) over the long term. I recommend spending a little of your marketing budget to hire a professional SEO expert. And I recommend you get a book or two on SEO to learn some of the basic terms and strategies. That way you can communicate your goals effectively to your SEO consultant, or even do a little keyword research on your own.

Free online directories. Many *online directories* will list your child care business free of charge or for a nominal fee of less than $50 per year. Some online directories are child care specific, and others are general in nature. The child care specific online directories are great because they already reach your intended target market: parents seeking child care.

Here is a list of some major online directories where you can list your program. Some are free, and some have a small annual fee.

- ChildCare Aware: www.childcareaware.org
- Great Schools: www.greatschools.org
- Care.com: www.care.com
- Daycare.com: www.daycare.com
- DaycareMatch: www.daycarematch.com
- The Daycare Resource Connection: www.daycareresource.com
- Daycare Hotline: www.daycarehotline.com
- Childcare-Directory: www.childcare-directory.com
- Daycare Bear: www.daycarebear.com
- MasterMOZ: www.mastermoz.com

(Note: Depending on when you are reading this book, some of the above sites may have ceased operation.)

Article marketing. *Article marketing* consists of writing articles about a topic and posting them to article websites. These articles may be written by you or one of your staff members on any number of early childhood topics—behavior problems, potty training, meal ideas, craft ideas, parenting tips, and so on. There are numerous article directory websites that accept articles from anyone who wants to post one.

Articles are a great way to get more exposure for your program on the Internet, to position yourself as an expert, and to generate inbound links. And you can leverage the articles you write by submitting them to offline publications like *Exchange* magazine or your local community magazine too. When you write an article, position yourself—or your program, or your teachers—as the expert on a particular topic. At the end of the article, include a brief biography of yourself, incorporating information about your program and, of course, a link to your business's website. Once posted, these articles will drive traffic to your website and often count as an inbound link, which in turn drives up your local SEO rankings.

> **TIP:** The web has many article sites. Here are a few I've used: http://ezinearticles.com, www.ehow.com, http://goarticles.com, and www.selfgrowth.com.

On a related note, you can also offer articles to your local media outlets who may be looking for family-oriented content. You might even be able to score a regular spot as the "local child care adviser"! Be sure to include your contact information and website address in every article you submit. Readers of the article who want to learn more about you will then be able to visit your website or schedule a visit.

Paid Traffic Sources

You may want to invest a little into *paid traffic sources*. By using basic website tracking programs like AWStats (http://awstats.sourceforge.net) or Google Analytics (www.google.com/analytics), it's usually pretty easy to measure which traffic sources are generating the highest level of targeted leads for your program so you can make sure you're getting the biggest bang for your marketing buck. Here are the most common paid traffic sources:

- pay-per-click (PPC) ads
- banner ads
- fee-based directories

Pay-per-click advertising. *Pay-per-click (PPC) advertising* is just what it sounds like—companies pay a certain amount each time someone clicks on their ad. Most search engines— for example, Google and Yahoo!—show their pay-per-click ads on the right-hand side (or sometimes at the top) of every web page you encounter when you do a search. If you've optimized your website for free traffic and used all the free strategies mentioned earlier, you can now experiment with driving more traffic to your site using PPC.

To begin your PPC advertising campaign, first set up an account with Google, Yahoo!, or whatever search engine you want to advertise on. You will be able to set a maximum daily budget as well as a maximum amount you are willing to spend per click. The maximum amount you are willing to spend is called your *cost-per-click*. Competing rates among advertisers for cost-per-click vary by market—that is, you may pay more for really competitive terms like "weight loss," or in large markets like Chicago.

I recommend you try to pay as little as possible per click. A reasonable rate in today's child care market is fifty cents or less per click. For example, if you set a daily budget of $5 and get a cost-per-click of 50 cents, you'll then get a maximum of ten leads per day to your site. A proportion of those who click on your ad (also known as a "sponsored listing") will be interested in your business, and if your website is doing its job, they'll sign up to receive more information or even call for a tour. Some of the clicks you pay for, however, will move away after landing at your site, which is to be expected; many folks simply surf the web and aren't part of your target audience.

As a general rule, I don't recommend child care leaders spend a lot of their marketing budget on PPC, because a lot of great traffic and leads can be generated by the free traffic-driving methods already discussed. If, however, your program is in a very competitive market and it's difficult for you to get onto

Google's page 1 using your keywords, then PPC can be a very effective strategy, because your target market will more easily find your website.

Banner ads. You can purchase *banner ads* on child care websites or other popular sites in your town or region that will drive traffic to your site. An example of this is a coupon site, where consumers can access and print coupons for all sorts of local businesses—restaurants, salons, retail shops, and child care centers. The fees for banner ads vary widely and are usually based on the volume of traffic generated on the website you're interested in.

When you begin to explore publishing a banner ad with a particular site, the most important metric to inquire about is the quantity of "unique visitors" it receives, rather than the number of hits or pageviews it receives. A unique visitor is just what it sounds like—one unique individual. When one unique individual goes to one web page, that's a pageview—if she clicked all five pages of your site, for example, that one visitor would represent five pageviews. If she returns later and visits those pages multiple times during the month, those translate to hits. So, as you can see, the metrics of hits and pageviews can be inflated.

If, for example, a person visits a website twice in a given month and clicks five pages in that site each time, that person could account for ten pageviews and fifty hits, even though she's just one unique visitor. A banner ad that is clicked by ten thousand unique visitors per month as opposed to one that receives ten thousand hits per month could mean substantial traffic for your site, especially if the hosting site is a local or regional one.

 To tell their unique story, Tom and Juanita created a new website that looked current and had great messaging. They automated their prospect follow-up by using a new e-mail management tool. Their final step was to make a plan for driving targeted traffic to their newly updated website. Tom, who was somewhat of a video junkie, was always making home movies. He used his video camera to begin filming footage of his teachers in action, as well as grabbing a few parents to do ad hoc video testimonials. He then created a YouTube channel for his school and uploaded all his videos to the channel. He also featured his video testimonials on his website. In addition, Tom and Juanita started tracking their Google and Yahoo! search results for their top keywords. They asked their website company to help them rank higher on Google and ended up ranking in the top three for most of their keyword phrases. They noticed that the proportion of inquiries who said they came from "the web" or "Google" was higher this quarter than it had been previously, and overall, their number of inquiries and tours was up.

Local child care is one of the top business categories young parents are searching for on the Internet. Many parents even preshop by researching on the web and whittling down their decision to tour just the top two or three programs based on what they find online. If you think it's not important to have a well-designed website that communicates your unique benefits and how much your customers love you, you are sorely mistaken. Further, your site must be findable by online searchers—otherwise you'll be like the proverbial tree that falls in the forest and no one ever hears it.

17

Online Media: Social Media

As I write this book, online *social media* is a growing phenomenon that is quickly becoming a mainstream method for businesses—child care professionals among them—to stay in touch with customers and prospects, to stay informed of the latest news and trends, and to generate new inquiries. The risk in writing about social media is that the medium is changing and morphing so quickly, this chapter is sure to be outdated in a matter of months. Even so, social media is an important trend in child care marketing, and the information that follows will give you an idea of how to use and leverage social media in your business-building efforts. Let's learn more about the advantages of using social media as one of your primary six media choices, and discover its disadvantages too.

Facebook

Right now, Facebook (www.facebook.com) is the most popular social networking site in the world, with over 750 million active users as of August 2011. People of all ages from around the globe are using Facebook to communicate with old friends and make new ones. One of the most popular features of Facebook is its easy photo-sharing capability, and this is what makes Facebook a good fit for child care businesses. You can use Facebook to post photographs taken at events at your facility or out in the community, and you can choose whether to share the photos with a private group of friends, such as current parent-clients, or to broaden the reach of your photos to the general public. (Note: When posting photos of children, you should obtain prior consent from parents in the form of a signed authorization agreeing to this activity on behalf of their child.)

To use Facebook for your child care program, you will need to set up a Facebook page (also known as a fan page). As of the publication date of this book, these pages are completely free—all you need to get started is a Facebook account. Once your page is set up, you can begin driving traffic to it by letting your existing parent-clients know that you have a new Facebook page and asking them to become "fans" and to demonstrate that they "like" your page. Communicate this information to parents in as many forms as you can: via e-mail, in your newsletter, in person, and also by posting flyers around your program. Give parents a good reason they should "like" your page: what photos and info will they be able to see and share? Then, as you make posts on your page by adding content and photos over time, customers and prospects will get into the habit of visiting your page and engaging with you via Facebook. Ideas for posts include fun things that are happening within your center, how your program is celebrating current or upcoming holidays, and enrollment promotions or specials you are offering.

Another great idea is to become a fan of or to "like" the Facebook pages of your community partners and to get them to "like" your page. When you do, you're cross-promoting each other in yet another medium, and you're continuing to reach the customers of other businesses that share your target audience (young families), not to mention engaging with the friends, neighbors, and coworkers of your current parent-clients.

A possible disadvantage to using Facebook to promote your business is that your Facebook page could be connected to someone who inadvertently uses offensive language or displays offensive behavior on the site. If your teachers are fans of your site, and one of them displays a photo of her new tattoo, for instance, it could have a negative impact on your program. The good news is you can delete other people's posts on your Facebook page, so you do have some control. Be cautious as you explore this growing phenomenon, and keep an eye on your Facebook page by monitoring it regularly.

Twitter

Another popular social networking site is Twitter (www.twitter.com). The premise of Twitter is that users follow each other to stay in touch about what they're doing in the moment. As of the publication date of this book, Twitter is free to join. All you need to do to get started is sign up for an account. Twitter can help you network with people, such as business partners, existing clients, and prospects; they follow you, and you can follow them. Many business owners who like Twitter use it to deepen their connection with their target audience—in your case, parents of young children. For example, you can send messages (called "tweets") about current events, trends, opinions, events, ideas, tips, or advice for parents of young children.

While I don't know many child care leaders who are currently using Twitter to network with friends, clients, and partners, this growing medium is sure to evolve.

More Social Media

Here are a few more social networking sites you might be interested in to help build the enrollment of your child care program and promote your business effectively online. Keep in mind that most of these sites are free to use and get listed on, which makes online social media a very cost-effective way to build relationships with current clients as well as find new ones.

YouTube

YouTube (www.youtube.com) allows users to create their own YouTube "channel" and then upload videos for friends or the world to view. This is a great way to showcase your program, build traffic, and increase customer loyalty. Ideas for videos you can post to your YouTube channel include parent and teacher testimonials, snippets of events going on in your program, field trips, virtual tours of your program, or a welcome message from the director or owner. For each video posted on YouTube, you can create a link back to your home page, which will help drive traffic to your website and improve your search engine rankings. (Google gives bonus points to websites that post videos through

YouTube, since Google owns YouTube.) Can you begin to see how all of your online marketing works together and can be leveraged?

LinkedIn

The primary purpose of LinkedIn (www.linkedin.com) is to enable people to network with others in their profession or line of work. You can use LinkedIn to network with other child care leaders, find top-notch employees, ask questions and get answers about a professional work situation or other topic, and touch base with former colleagues.

Squidoo

Squidoo (www.squidoo.com) allows users to publish their own pages on niche topics (each page is called a "lens") designed to attract readers and even earn a little money. Advertisers like Google can be integrated into your lens, and if your lens makes money, Squidoo will split the commissions with you fifty-fifty. You can collect the money via Paypal (www.paypal.com) or opt to donate it to your favorite charity. As a child care leader, you could create a lens on an aspect of early childhood learning (such as your favorite curriculum ideas), or any number of topics related either to child care or a personal interest of yours. Lenses are rated and ranked, so if your lens becomes popular, it can generate buzz for your program. It can also generate new Facebook friends or fans, new Twitter followers, and new YouTube viewers.

Consumer Review Sites: Yelp, SavvySource, and GreatSchools

Online review sites are places on the Internet where consumers can post their opinions about a local business, a product, or a service. Some of the most popular review sites where parents actively post reviews of child care programs include Yelp (www.yelp.com), SavvySource (www.savvysource.com), and GreatSchools (www.greatschools.org). It's a best practice to consistently monitor these sites to keep an eye on what parents are saying about your child care program, as well as those of your competitors. Many programs receive an occasional negative review by a disgruntled employee or parent, but your reviews should be heavily weighted with glowing remarks and positive testimonials.

Social media have two primary disadvantages, as I see it: it's difficult to directly measure the return on investment of your efforts, and it can take a lot of time to stay connected on all the different forms of social media. You can measure the number of Facebook fans you have and how many people have viewed your videos on YouTube, but how do you directly translate those numbers to leads, tours, and enrollments? I'm not aware of any easy tactics to help you measure the revenue impact of social media sites on your child care business.

However, there is still value in social media, if only because it's where your target market congregates, and it's a place for you to deepen your connection and strengthen your loyalty fence with customers, alumni, prospects, and partners. Use the following exercise to brainstorm ways you can use and leverage these social networking opportunities.

> **TIP:** I created some special bonus gifts just for readers of this book. For a free guide on how to address negative online reviews and how to lessen their impact on your program, go to www.child caremarketingbook.com.

Exercise 18 Brainstorm Ways to Use and Leverage Online Social Media

Here is a list of the six social media sites we just learned about. Brainstorm ways that your program can use and leverage each of these as part of your marketing plan.

1. Facebook: _____

_____

_____

_____

2. Twitter: _____

_____

_____

3. YouTube: _____

_____

_____

4. LinkedIn: _____

_____

_____

5. Squidoo: _____

_____

_____

6. Review sites: _____

_____

_____

Tom and Juanita had to admit it—they were not at all excited about the idea of social networking online. Neither of them personally used Facebook or Twitter, and neither had any desire to. However, they knew parents of young children congregated on these sites—and several parents had been asking Juanita if she was on Facebook. They agreed to start their social media journey by dipping their toe in the water and learning more over the next three months. They talked to their assistant director about doing social media training sessions. They included social media integration in their marketing plan to take place around six months from now.

Whether you do your own social media updates and connections or delegate it to another person on your staff, it's an important part of your marketing arsenal.

18

Community Marketing

Community marketing consists of any strategy you use to personally connect with local residents and business partners, such as participation in local events, cross-promotional campaigns with other businesses, and membership in community organizations. I always recommend that my clients utilize community marketing strategies, especially those who own or manage a new child care program just getting started. The reason? Perhaps the number one method for child care business owners and directors to quickly build their program's enrollment is to introduce themselves to and make connections with as many community members as possible. Case in point: One of my clients personally visited local businesses every day for thirty days, after which she opened her new child care program fully enrolled with a waiting list. She got out of her comfort zone and made community connections and, as a result, quickly generated massive word of mouth.

Another great way for child care programs to build their enrollment is to participate in community events, particularly those that draw families with young children. My hometown has three big annual events that draw hundreds, if not thousands, of families with young children. Many of the early childhood businesses sponsor booths at these events because it's a natural fit for engaging with local families. Here are some ideas for local events you can and should participate in:

- art and music fairs
- food and wine events

- neighborhood-sponsored carnivals
- neighborhood holiday parades (Memorial Day or the Fourth of July, for example)
- holiday events, such as Santa and Mrs. Claus appearances
- fundraising or charitable events
- family fun runs

At these types of events, most organizers will provide exhibiting businesses a skirted table and a couple of chairs. Find out what items are included with your booth sponsorship so you can plan accordingly. Think about events you've attended and what kinds of exhibits have been the most appealing—what can you offer at your booth that will draw in families? Some of the best ideas I've used are children's games ("fish" to win a prize, bean bag toss, and so on) and a prize wheel that passersby can spin to win. As they spin the wheel or play the game, you can find out about their child care needs and present the benefits of your program. Bring marketing materials—brochures, flyers, enrollment coupons, even a laptop loaded with a slide show of photographs—that give attendees more information about your program.

When you participate in any community event, have a system for capturing the names and information of all the parents (and children) who visit your booth so that you can follow up with them. An event marketing expert once told me that his rule of thumb is 10 percent of event attendees will be actively seeking the service or product you offer, 20 percent will never be interested, and the remaining 70 percent will likely be interested sometime in the future. This means you must have a system for following up with local family leads you get from the event. You can gather names and addresses most effectively by offering some type of prize drawing or sweepstakes that parents can enter. Make the prize something that has great appeal to your target audience. Prize ideas can include the following:

- a family travel voucher for air travel or hotel
- a large outdoor playset or climber
- an art easel and art set
- a family zoo membership
- a tech gadget, such as an e-book reader or MP3 player

After the event is over, create a follow-up campaign to reach the prospective families who visited your booth. (Use the ideas provided in chapter 20 on direct mail to fuel your creative follow-up campaign.) At the very least, send a handwritten note or letter thanking them for coming by your booth, mentioning how nice it was to meet them and their kids, and offering them an enrollment special or coupon with a deadline date for taking action. You could also invite them to come say hello, take a tour, and receive a special free gift for their children. Yet another idea is to ask them to provide the date of their child's birthday on your booth information form, and send out birthday cards to those children throughout the year. This will make a tremendous impact on families—the fact that you followed through and actually took the time to send a birthday card and note. Take it one step further and send an inexpensive children's book to the child. Now that's an unusual marketing approach that will definitely get noticed and set you apart from your competitors!

Take the following steps to get the most impact from local events.

1. Obtain a list from your Chamber of Commerce or another source of all the local events planned for your area, and if you have a lot of customers from an adjacent town, get their list as well.
2. Choose three to five events to participate in, based on price, expected attendance, and likely target audience. (For example, stay away from events like the Senior Golf Tournament.)
3. Map out the events scheduled to occur for the next nine to twelve months on your calendar.
4. Contact the event organizers and let them know you'd like to participate.

Consider these factors when deciding what events to participate in:

- Cost: What is the cost to participate in each event compared to what you will receive for participating? Typically, the larger the event (and the bigger the draw), the more it will cost to exhibit. Compare your top three to five choices in terms of cost versus anticipated benefit.
- Attendee quantity and type: Ask the event organizer for information on how many people typically attend the event, and of those,

what proportion are families with young children. Put your time and energy into the events that draw good traffic and where you can connect with your target audience.

- Event theme: What is the overall style or theme of this event? Is it a good fit for your message or what you plan to offer at your booth? How can you tie into the theme to leverage your participation?
- Timing of event: Is the event indoors or outdoors? What will the weather be like in your area at that time? Is the event well timed to when people are typically thinking about summer or fall enrollment or other busy enrollment periods for your program?
- Personnel scheduling: Who will staff the event? What else is going on in your program or their calendar that might be a schedule conflict?

Another way to tie into an event is to offer drop-in child care at the event. For example, if your town's retailers host a holiday shopping night or other couples events, offer to provide the child care for the event. Set up a simple but fun play area within another business—perhaps that of a community partner—or reserve a community room at your library. This is a great way to get good local publicity, and all of the retailers will love you for it, because then the parents can spend more time shopping! Provide a simple authorization form for parents to note any special concerns, such as food allergies or diapering instructions. And get the full contact information for the family so you can follow up with them after the event. When parents return to pick them up, give the children a balloon or fruit snack with your logo on it.

Now that you've gotten a good sense of how to evaluate different events, use the following exercise to research, select, and staff your chosen events by creating your plan and adding them to your program calendar.

Exercise 19 Create a Community Event Plan and Calendar

Complete the steps in this exercise to create your community event plan and calendar.

1. Contact all the community organizations in your town (Chamber of Commerce, Kiwanis, parents groups, and so on) and ask for their event calendars. Often you

can do most of this research online, as many business groups now post their full calendar of events on their websites.

2. Choose a number of community events from this master list that fit your program and your budget. A good number is three to five solid events for the year that appeal to you in terms of target market, theme, size, and date.

3. Grab your calendar of events for your center or school, and pencil in the dates of the community events. Are there any potential conflicts or staffing concerns? If so, address those.

4. Contact the event organizers about three months in advance of the event's date and let them know you'd like to participate.

In addition to participating in events, leverage community ties through your marketing by developing cross-promotional campaigns with partners. One client of mine did this very effectively. She heard about a new children's soccer program starting in her town and approached the program director to see whether she would be willing to cross-promote her business. My client received a positive response, so she started including the soccer program brochure in all her prospect information packets—the folders she gave prospective parents during a center tour. In exchange, the soccer program also promoted and recommended her child care program to parents. Both businesses received new customers as a result.

 Tom and Juanita were members of their local chamber as well as the Rotary Club. They began their event planning process by contacting those groups and looking for events they could exhibit at. They created an event planning calendar. Juanita had heard about a Moms with Tots group (with about 150 local moms), so she made a connection with them and learned that they had an annual event as well as a monthly newsletter that she could advertise in. By regularly going to chamber and rotary meetings, Tom found several fellow business owners who wanted to promote ABC Learning Center in exchange for Tom's promoting their business. Tom and Juanita's community marketing activities started gaining momentum.

By creating and actively working your plan, you will get out of reactive mode in your event planning and partnership-building. You will begin taking full advantage of all the community marketing opportunities—even some that you may not be aware of at this point.

19

Publicity Campaigns

One of the best ways to get the word out about your child care center or school is to get your local media outlets—newspapers, magazines, radio and television stations—to give you *publicity*. To use this strategy, you simply identify newsworthy stories about your child care program or events that you're participating in and send out press releases about them. The big benefit of local publicity is that it is completely free, and it's a great way to reach a huge number of people in your market. What could be better?

Here are five great tips for getting more local publicity for your child care program:

Leverage an existing event or cause. The owners of one child care center I work with are members of their local Rotary Club. They came up with the idea to leverage a Santa and Mrs. Claus event by cohosting a raffle at the event to benefit the local Rotary Club. The child care business raised over $1,300 by selling raffle tickets to local families to win a Little Tikes deluxe playhouse while they waited in line with their children to see Santa and Mrs. Claus. The owners had written a simple press release to promote the raffle ahead of the event; after the raffle was over, they wrote another press release to announce the winner and report how much money was raised. As a result, this program received two articles in back-to-back editions of the local paper, just from this one event! The word of mouth they received from the media coverage was tremendous.

Organize a food, clothing, or toy drive. This idea is similar to the one above and is a great way to give back to those in your community who are less fortunate.

Before the event, write a press release with the details of the food, clothing, or toy drive, and send it to your local media; after the event, write and send another one to communicate how much food or clothing or how many toys were collected and donated. Provide the recipient organization—women's shelters, animal shelters, literacy programs, or children's services organizations—with plenty of information about your child care business, and leave some flyers or brochures with them when you drop off the donations.

Join local business organizations. Publicity photos and news coverage of local groups like the Kiwanis, Rotary, Chamber of Commerce, or Lions Club is very common. You can get your business's name and your or a staff member's photo in the paper simply by being a member of these organizations. Membership is also a great way to network with other business owners in your town!

Sponsor a booth at a local event. This opportunity was covered in detail in chapter 18. Get your calendar and map out all the local community events that attract families during the year, such as spring flings, summer carnivals, fall harvest fests, and Santa events. Contact the sponsors of these events and host a booth with children's activities, such as face painting, crafts, and games. While your program is not guaranteed to receive publicity just by being at the event, chances are good that your local newspaper will be there taking photos, and you might just land on the front page of your local paper. You can also provide a press release giving details about what's happening at your booth or what big giveaways you are doing.

Offer drop-in child care at a local event. This idea was also mentioned in the previous chapter and is a great way to get local publicity. All the retailers will love you for it, because when parents have quality child care available, parents can shop more! Again, if you offer this service, make sure your business name and your donated service are mentioned in any articles promoting the event in advance—this will drive up event attendance and gain you free media exposure at the same time.

Have fun with these ideas, and be sure to take action by getting out your calendar and making a publicity plan to get the most "bang" for your participation in local events and fundraisers. Use the following exercise to get started.

Exercise 20 Brainstorm Ways to Gain Publicity

For each of the following seven categories, brainstorm ways you can generate publicity. Make note of the topic to be covered in a press release, when the information should be released, and who it will be sent to.

1. Fundraising events: _____

_____

_____

_____

2. Charitable donation drives: _____

_____

_____

_____

3. In-center events: _____

_____

_____

_____

4. Community events we are participating in: _____

_____

_____

_____

_____

_____

5. Holiday celebrations (such as planting trees on Earth Day): _____

_____

_____

_____

6. Special enrollment promotions: _____

_____

_____

_____

7. Other ideas: _____

_____

_____

_____

_____

> **TIP:** Never written a press release? No problem. For a free press release template and example you can adapt, visit www.childcaremarket ingbook.com.

 Tom and Juanita made a list of all the newsworthy events, donation drives, and fun holiday-related promotions they were planning for the coming year. They contacted all their local media representatives to find out how each one wanted to receive press releases—most gave an e-mail address, but some wanted to receive the press releases via fax. Using their media list and their list of topics, they set a goal to write and submit at least one press release each month to keep their program top-of-mind with local residents.

Publicity is a fantastic medium, because in general, people enjoy reading features about and seeing photos of young children. Plus, of course, you can't beat the affordability of it. Using publicity as one of the tools in your marketing arsenal will help your program increase awareness in the community, stay top-of-mind with prospects and customers, and help you forge more partnerships in the community.

CHAPTER

20

Direct Mail

As a media choice, *direct mail* includes any marketing message you would mail directly to your customer's or prospect's home or workplace, in the form of a letter, postcard, greeting card, thank-you note, or even a gift package. In my opinion, direct mail gets a bad rap, and unnecessarily so. Most child care business owners and directors are reluctant to use direct mail because they may have tried it once and it didn't work; now they see it as only a huge waste of money. What I propose is a very different approach to direct mail than what most child care leaders have tried. Please keep an open mind.

Why Use Direct Mail?

Here are a few important reasons why direct mail can be highly effective, and why you should give it serious consideration:

It's highly targeted. Direct mail is a great way to reach your target market, because it is exactly that: extremely targeted. You can purchase or rent lists drawing from many different demographic and geographic characteristics, for example, the age of children in the home, what magazines the parents subscribe to, and families who have recently moved into a specific zip code or neighborhood, among many others.

Everyone gets mail. Not everyone watches TV, reads the local paper, owns a computer, or listens to a particular radio station, so there can be a lot of waste in traditional media. But everyone gets mail and can be reached in that manner.

Everyone looks at direct mail. Studies have shown that looking through their pile of mail is one of the first things people do when they get home from work. (It's right up there with going to the bathroom!)

It's easy to make direct mail stand out. When you create your direct mail pieces, be a little daring—outrageous even—to grab the attention of your prospect so that she simply cannot resist opening your mail and reading the headline. If you make your direct mail piece look like it's from a friend or neighbor, for example, by actually hand-addressing the piece and using a postage stamp, it's also much more likely to get opened. Another great way to make sure your mailer gets opened is to use three-dimensional (3-D) or lumpy mail. (More on 3-D mail later in this chapter.)

You can personalize direct mail. Direct mail is the only medium other than e-mail that allows you to personalize your message by using the prospect's name in the letter and throughout the mailer. You can also refer to the street she lives on or the town she lives in. And depending on the data you collect or have access to, you can send a prospect mail on her birthday, her children's birthdays, or her anniversary. You can also do a neighbor-to-neighbor campaign, where you refer to the name of one of the prospect's neighbors who uses your child care program—ideally accompanied by a glowing testimonial from that neighbor about your program!

It's a great way to test marketing elements. Direct mail is perhaps the best medium to use to test different elements of your marketing message. For example, if you have a list of five hundred prospects, you can create one overall mail piece but test two different offers—you could send one offer to half of the prospects and the same piece with a different offer to the other half. You can then see which offer is more appealing based on your response levels. Be sure when doing this type of test that you change only one aspect of the mailer. If you change both the headline and the offer, for instance, you won't know which element caused a difference in response.

For all of these reasons, direct mail is one of my favorite mediums to use to help child care programs get more prospects and enrollments. But don't waste your money sending one-shot direct mail. For best results, I recommend setting up a sequential mailing campaign.

Sequential Mailings: Multistep Campaigns

Sequential mail campaigns are a series of mailings that are sent to the same list of people each time. There are usually three or more "steps," or mailings, per campaign, each of which is mailed in fairly quick succession so that prospects and customers receive something from you regularly. The goal of sequential mailing is to stay top-of-mind with your prospects and customers. For example, you might send a letter with a promotional enrollment offer to the Smith family; this mailing would be the first step. Then, ten days later, you would send them a follow-up postcard referring back to the first letter and ask, "Why haven't I heard from you yet?"; this mailing would be the second step. Then, two weeks down the road, you would send the Smiths a third letter extending yet another special last-chance enrollment offer, making sure to highlight the deadline date; this mailing would be the third step.

In many types of enterprises, including early childhood businesses, sequential mailings have proven to be more effective than one-shot mailers. In many cases, I've seen the results from steps two and three, taken together, outperform the results of step one. So if you mailed out five hundred pieces and received ten inquiries from step one, in a sequential mailing you would typically receive an additional ten inquiries—possibly more—from steps two and three combined.

> **TIP:** To receive free samples of direct mail campaigns that have worked to bring new inquiries and enrollments to child care programs, please visit www .childcaremarketingbook.com.

When measuring the success of your sequential-mailing campaign, focus on the return on investment, or ROI, rather than the response rate or response percentage. For example, if you spent $1,500 to print and mail out those five hundred pieces in a three-step campaign, and you converted the twenty inquiries generated into three new enrollments, you should look at the annual revenue or the lifetime customer value, the LCV, from those new enrollments to determine your ROI on the campaign. If your annual revenue for three new enrolling families is an additional $15,000, and the campaign cost you $1,500 total, then you would have a 10-to-1 return on your investment; that is, for every dollar you invested in the campaign, you earned back $10 in revenue.

3-D ("Lumpy") Mail

Three-dimensional (3-D) mail, or *lumpy mail*, is a great technique to use to make sure your piece actually gets opened. Three-dimensional mail creates curiosity, making it hard to resist opening the envelope. Sometimes the item that's inside the envelope is 3-D, such as a pacifier or a package of aspirin affixed to the top of a letter. Another approach is to mail your message in something other than an envelope to get it opened. I've seen a wallet mailer, a bank-bag mailer, a trash-can mailer, even a coconut! You really can mail just about anything through the U.S. Postal Service. When people get a bank bag or a colored tube in the mail, do you think they can resist opening it up? Would you? Again, the goal of using 3-D mail is to get your piece opened and read by your prospect.

To make your 3-D mailing most effective, use the theme of your message to match the lumpy item or mailer. For example, if you mail a pacifier in your letter, your headline could read, "When You Realize How Happy Your Child Will Be in Our Program, You'll Sleep Like a Baby." I recommend talking to your local direct mail expert to get ideas and guidance on how to cost effectively use 3-D mail and to make sure you are meeting any postal rules and regulations.

TIP: For great ideas on how to use 3-D Mail, including a free DVD with examples of direct mail campaigns and letters you can adapt, go to www.3DMailResults.com.

Who Should Be Getting Your Mail?

You should be mailing to three different groups of people: current customers, past customers, and prospects.

Current Customers

One benefit of sending direct mail to your current customers is that it can strengthen your loyalty fence. Use it to remind them from time to time of your referral-rewards program. If you have a monthly newsletter (which I hope you do), you should be mailing it to the homes of all your current clients. Doing so will get you a much higher readership than if you put it in their child's cubby at school. One school owner I work with uses a program called SendOutCards (www.SendOutCards.com) to automatically send personalized cards, such as birthday and anniversary cards, to current customers. It's automated, so all you have to do is load in the addresses and dates—the system does the rest.

Sending direct mail to your current customers can be a fabulous way to build a tight rapport with them and to inspire them to spread positive word-of-mouth publicity about your program.

Past Customers

Past customers (who already know, trust, and love you) can be a great source for new business. Use direct mail to touch base with them. Tell them about new things going on in your program—a new referral-rewards program, perhaps—or invite parents and children to an upcoming event.

One early childhood program owner I know used this technique to fill her summer camp. Using a three-step sequential mail campaign (all three steps were postcards or greeting cards sent to graduates of her program) she offered a 10 percent discount off each week of summer camp. She tracked the campaign by telling customers to mention the code "GRAD" when they called or enrolled.

Her campaign was tremendously successful! Of the 136 families she mailed to, 20 enrolled in her summer camp. She projected $35,000 in revenue during the summer and spent only $500 on the entire campaign. That's a 70-to-1 return on investment!

Prospects

Direct mail can help you generate prospects. You can purchase or rent mailing lists based on a variety of demographic, geographic, and psychographic factors (such as subscriber lists or compiled lists based on past purchases). If you live in a densely populated area, a great way to get a high-quality mailing list is to create a database in a spreadsheet program of your current and past clients. A direct mail company can profile the list to identify your typical customer to find new prospects like them.

Be bold when you mail to a list of prospects that may not know you. Use the 3-D mail techniques to get your letter opened. Use a benefit-driven or emotion-based headline to grab your prospects' attention right away. Use lots of testimonials and rave reviews to let them know that other moms and dads love the service you provide. Use engaging photos of children. Make a strong, high-value special offer with a deadline attached to enroll or take a tour. Use something free to entice them into taking action. Then use SendOutCards to automatically send follow-up cards a week or so after a tour.

> **TIP:** The largest list broker in the United States is InfoUSA. Contact them to inquire about profiling your list or to find out what kinds of prospect lists are available. For more information, go to www.infousa.com.

 Tom and Juanita had gathered over two hundred names and addresses of prospects who had toured with them in the last eighteen months, but they had never done anything with the information. They compiled the names and addresses into an Excel spreadsheet and called a direct mail firm to help them figure out how to best take advantage of this untapped asset for their business. The direct mail company input the names and addresses of ABC's customers and prospects into a profiling software application, which was able to produce "matches" of other families in their draw area who looked similar—demographically and geographically—to their existing customers and prospects. The profiling software located about 325 more families with young children who matched their current target audience.

Tom and Juanita were excited to start sending fun, personality-oriented cards, letters, and postcards to their target prospects—both the 200 families who had toured them in the past, as well as the 325 new records. They used a three-step mail campaign that hit the mailboxes of their prospects three times right before heavy enrollment season: late July, early August, and mid-August. They received ten inquiries from a three-sequence 500-piece mail campaign, for a 2 percent response rate overall. Even more important, they converted six of those inquiries to enrollments, for a total of nine new children in their program.

Many small business owners I know personally have become hugely successful and wealthy by studying the art and science of direct mail, and testing new ideas to improve response rates and ROI over time. With a little persistence and creativity, your child care program can achieve phenomenal results with enrollment building by mastering the use of direct mail in your marketing tool kit.

21

Local Media Advertising

As a small business owner or manager, you probably do not have a massive marketing budget to spend on brand advertising or glitzy network television media campaigns. You need be able to measure the results of your marketing dollars and to have them work hard and smart for you by making your phone ring. For these reasons, I guide my clients toward direct-response strategies in local media. *Direct response* means your ad always includes a call to action for readers so they will respond directly to you. Usually, the call to action in your direct-response advertisement would be to respond to your special offer, free gift, or informational report—something of value to your target audience.

Here are some ground rules for using local advertising media effectively for your program:

- Choose the most highly targeted media you can find, or ask for placement in a section or segment that is popular with parents of young children. For example, if your region has a magazine specifically for young families, that may be a better media choice than a general-interest local newspaper.
- Always use as many of the eight key ingredients of good messaging (from chapter 13) as possible in your ads: headline, offer, deadline, benefits, unique value statement, guarantee, testimonials, and a unique identifier.
- Be a little outrageous. It's okay—even desirable—to be unique and different in your approach to your marketing. You don't want to be boring or to look the same as all your competitors. You need to

make your advertising memorable to cut through the clutter of all the thousands of messages people get hit with every week. Your photos, headline, copy, guarantee, and testimonials should make your target audience perk up and take notice.

The disadvantage to using local media is that they are not as targeted as direct mail, e-mail, community family events, or even your website is. That's because it's hard to reach just your target market (young families in a particular zip code or area of town) when you advertise in a local newspaper or magazine, or on radio or television. And the advertising rates for these local media outlets are based on the total number of eyeballs reached—not just the eyeballs of your target market. Said another way, there can be a lot of waste when you advertise in local media, unless it is a niche publication. On the other hand, if your local newspaper is offering a special editorial section on trends in child care or a special summer camp issue, you may find this type of targeted opportunity will perform better for your business.

Lead Generation Advertising

Lead generation advertising is sometimes referred to as two-step marketing because it offers the prospect a free or low-cost item of value to get her to "raise her hand" to show interest in what your ad is offering. For example, if you offered a free guide on "How to Choose the Right Preschool" to readers of a mom-oriented publication, you might ask them to call an 800 number or go to a certain web page to obtain the report. This allows you to generate a lead—hence, the reason it's called lead generation advertising. So the first step is generating the lead and gaining the prospect's contact information. It's now up to you to implement the second step—contacting her with reasons for visiting your program—and then creating a follow-up campaign with as many steps as needed to gain her trust and enrollment.

Why should you consider lead generation advertising rather than just advertising your program like everyone else? Mainly because it's more attractive to your prospect to take action to get something of value to her and her family—especially if it's free or low cost—than it is simply to call your program and take the tour. With this method, you are building your prospect list and building a trusted relationship with the people on that list, not just selling them your service. Can you see the distinction and how that sets your program apart in the marketplace?

Here are some additional ideas for lead generation ads:

Tie in to a newsworthy event or situation on the minds of your target market. If everyone is talking about a new health scare, such as the H1N1 virus, offer a free report titled "Everything Parents Need to Know about H1N1 Virus." Ideally, this report would be written by you, the business owner or director, but you could also partner with a local hospital or pediatrician and coauthor the report. Tying your advertising to a newsworthy event is a great strategy for generating prospects because it allows you to enter the conversation already going on in the minds of your prospects. Plus, it can position you as the local expert in child-related issues—which after all, you are.

> **TIP:** For examples of lead generation ads you can adapt, please visit www.childcare marketingbook.com.

Offer a free gift of children's products and services, and advertise the retail value of the gift. One center I work with contacted their retail partners in the community and obtained children's items—T-shirts, books, and so on—that cross-promoted their partners' businesses. The retail value of the free gift was $479. The center offered the free gift in a lead generation ad in the local paper and got many calls from parents wanting more information as a result.

Exercise 21 Think about Local Media Advertising

Answer the following questions, which are designed to get you started on taking action on the ideas we've discussed in this chapter.

1. What traditional local media have you advertised in within the past two years, and how do you "guesstimate" that it performed for you in terms of generating inquiries?

_____

_____

_____

_____

2. Do some market research about what other targeted, family-oriented publications and media are available that you have not used in the past. Identify one or two that appeal to you and contact them to learn more about rates, audience size, demographics, any special issues, and so forth.

_____

_____

_____

_____

3. Talk to your business partners and network with local community groups. What local media have they used that was successful in bringing in new leads and customers?

_____

_____

_____

4. Brainstorm some ideas for lead generation ads. What free reports, parenting guides, or gifts can you offer that will get parents to "raise their hand" to take the next step with you?

_____

_____

_____

Juanita and Tom had never advertised in any local media—they just assumed it was too expensive and too hard to make an impact with their target customers. At one of their networking meetings with the Chamber of Commerce, they asked around and learned that one of their partners had some success advertising in a local magazine called *Family Matters*. Juanita and Tom decided to give it a try. They designed an ad to look like an article with the headline "Q&A with the Owners of ABC Learning Center." The copy included questions like, "What should local families consider when choosing a preschool?" At the end of the article, they provided an 800 number prospects could call to get a free "Summer Activity Guide." Juanita and Tom paid $125 for the half-page ad and received nine calls from families on the 800 number. By following up and sending the free guide along with a special enrollment offer, a brochure, and parent testimonials, they generated two new enrollments from this effort. Considering their annual enrollment revenue from these two new customer families, the ad had a very good return on investment. (As you will see in the next chapter, they decided to continue testing this media vehicle, and budgeted $250 in their quarterly marketing plan to test two more ads in this magazine over the next three months.)

We've now learned the advantages and disadvantages of six media choices: websites, social media, community marketing, publicity campaigns, direct mail, and local advertising. This is not an exclusive list—in addition to these six choices, you may find other media to test and use (such as billboards, creative signage, and so on). But by using these six effectively, you should find that you are reaching more of your target prospects and building your enrollment. Now let's learn about how to pull these six media choices together with a marketing budget.

CHAPTER

22

Develop Your Marketing Budget

You probably don't have a ton of money to spend—or waste—on massive image-oriented ads and brand advertising campaigns that look pretty but have no call to action. As a small business owner or director, you need to have a laserlike focus on targeted, cost-effective media that will cut through the clutter to reach your target market with messages that communicate your unique value statement and are backed up by social proof—testimonials, rave reviews, and your guarantee.

How much money should you spend on these media, and what's the best way to set your budget? A good rule of thumb, based on the experiences of early childhood businesses I've worked with, is to spend 2 percent to 4 percent of your projected quarterly gross revenue on marketing activities. So if your quarterly tuition revenue is $150,000, you would budget between $3,000 and $6,000 to spend on all your marketing and advertising activities. You may, of course, choose to allocate more or less, and that's fine.

 ABC Learning Center now has seventy-eight children enrolled (up from sixty-five), and its projected quarterly gross revenue is $116,000. (Its annual sales revenue is roughly $464,000 based on current enrollment.) Using 2 percent to 4 percent as the guideline, Tom and Juanita should spend from $2,300 to $4,600 this quarter on marketing, advertising, and promotion. They moved some expenses around so they could handle a solid marketing budget of $3,600. (Later on we will learn exactly how they are going to spend that budget.)

How does ABC Learning Center's media budget—$2,300 to $4,600 per quarter—compare to what you're spending right now on your media efforts? If this number seems really high to you, remember to consider the lifetime customer value of your average enrolled family.

 Tom and Juanita's LCV is $25,000 per family, so they are more than happy to invest about $3,000 per quarter on marketing and advertising their program to stay fully enrolled. After all, their return on investment is substantial—on average, they are spending about $500 to get a new family enrolled, and the average enrolling family is worth about $25,000 to their program. So their ROI is 50 to 1—for every dollar they spend, they receive $50 back in revenue. Tom and Juanita know that even if the effectiveness of their marketing declines and they get just one new family enrolled each month, their quarterly marketing investment will pay for itself many times over. They are also working to build up their retention rate of existing clients using improved customer service practices and a family appreciation program.

Now that you've seen how Tom and Juanita have determined how much they can afford to spend on their media each quarter, use the following exercise to determine your marketing budget.

Exercise 22 Determine Your Quarterly Marketing Budget

Complete the following steps. Feel free to adjust the time frame to monthly or annually, if that's more suited to your budgeting process.

1. Determine your projected quarterly gross revenue.   = _____

2. Calculate 2 percent of the amount in step 1.   = _____

3. Calculate 4 percent of the amount in step 1.   = _____

4. Range of budget to be allocated to marketing activities
   (range should be between the figures in steps 2 and 3).   = _____

Tom and Juanita took the next step in creating their marketing plan by allocating their $3,600 marketing budget to a broad menu of media choices they were excited to implement. Their plan included all but one of the six media types we covered in this section—the exception was social media. They plan to "eat the elephant one bite at a time" by entering the somewhat daunting world of social media sometime in the next six months. For now, they will focus on implementing all the marketing efforts shown in figure 22-1. Happily, Tom and Juanita no longer feel like marketing victims. Through their persistence and with the help of their friend Mark, they have transformed themselves little by little into marketing champions!

Figure 22-1: First Quarter (Jan–Mar): ABC Learning Center Marketing Budget

Marketing Element	Budget
Website and online marketing	$350
Community events/publicity campaign	200
Referral-rewards program	800
Direct mail	1,200
Local newspaper ads	250
Moms of Tots club newsletter ads	75
New signage	225
Flyers and brochures	500
TOTAL	**$3,600**

Use Tom and Juanita's example above to take the next step for your marketing plan. Carve out your marketing budget by determining what specific media you would like to use to promote and market your program. Get current rates from advertising vendors and event organizers. Don't worry: you may be stepping into new territory, but as you continue to track your return on investment for each effort and compare them to one another, you will start learning what's working best to bring in new enrollments. Be careful about making quick judgments about certain media versus others; look at the message you used in that particular activity and how much of your intended target market you actually reached. If you need more help tracking your return on investment by marketing activity, refer back to chapter 4.

When you get all four marketing pillars humming effectively—using *metrics* to track your effectiveness at getting the right *message* to the right *market* using the right *media*—you'll feel like a marketing champion, just as Tom and Juanita do!

Now Take Action!

☐ Complete the exercises right away.

☐ Research what your market reads, watches, listens to, or uses online, and plan your media choices accordingly.

☐ Have friends or colleagues "audit" your website to look for strengths and weaknesses. Make sure your contact info is on every page of the site.

☐ Once a month, do a local search on all the major search engines for child care in your town. Keep track of your result rankings for all your keyword phrases. If you're not in the top ten results, use search engine optimization techniques such as link-building and posting videos on YouTube to get your site ranked higher.

☐ Add a fun and charming video to your home page that communicates your unique benefits.

☐ Create your media budget on a quarterly basis. Make sure you can track the ROI for each effort so you know what's making your phone ring.

☐ Find out what media or local groups are reaching people moving into your town or region.

☐ Write a press release or two and submit them to your local newspaper.

☐ Plan a three-step sequential-mailing campaign to your best neighborhood. Mail to a small list of prospects (at least 250) in this neighborhood, and test your results.

☐ Offer a free report or a free child care checklist. Use lead generation advertising to get prospects to contact you to receive the free item.

Tools for Success: Plans and Systems

The course of true anything never does run smooth.
—SAMUEL BUTLER

Failure is the condiment that gives success its flavor.
—TRUMAN CAPOTE

23

Your Strategic Marketing Action Plan (S-MAP)

Congratulations! You've now learned about the four pillars of your child care marketing plan—metrics, market, message, and media—and you have more marketing knowledge than most early childhood professionals. If you've done the exercises in this book, then you've also developed some core business and marketing skills that will serve you for the rest of your career. You are well positioned to grow the enrollment of your child care program and secure its financial well-being.

Two important tools can help you take all that you've learned and translate it into action. The first tool is simply a *plan*. Have you heard the expression, "Plan the work and then work the plan"? Having a plan will keep you focused on where you need to take action to grow your enrollment and transform your child care business into a financially healthy one. And when you feel confused about what action to take, you can go back to your plan to redirect yourself.

The plan I have created for you to use as a template is called a *Strategic Marketing Action Plan,* or *S-MAP* for short. The S-MAP can be your road map for success, because it is specifically designed to walk you step-by-step through the important aspects of each marketing pillar to determine the best strategies and tactics for your program. (Of course, a marketing plan can take many different forms. As long as you find a plan format that works for you, that's fine.)

To learn more, let's walk through each section of the S-MAP now. Review the S-MAP template provided in appendix C. Then we'll use the one Tom and Juanita completed for their business as our example.

Section 1: SWOT Analysis

Section 1 of the S-MAP is a *SWOT analysis*. SWOT is your best take on what your program's current strengths, weaknesses, opportunities, and threats are. You may want to corral your staff and have them help you with this part of the exercise. Involving staff is a great opportunity to utilize team-building techniques and offers the chance to begin training them on your new approaches to marketing and enrollment building.

The value of a SWOT analysis is that it sets the foundation for strategic thinking and provides your team with the business- and market-based landscape that will greatly impact your program's future performance.

In figure 23-1, you can see the SWOT analysis for ABC Learning Center, where Tom and Juanita have determined their strengths, weaknesses, opportunities, and threats.

Figure 23-1: SWOT Analysis for ABC Learning Center

Section 1: SWOT Analysis

S: According to the voices of my customers, the key strengths of my program are:

Ethnically diverse family population; bilingual teaching (Spanish and English);

longevity in the community; excellent reputation; nationally accredited

W: According to the voices of my customers, the key weaknesses of my program are:

Lack of secure entrance to school; higher initial registration fees than competitors;

recent teacher turnover caused some turmoil

O: The key opportunities for my business to prosper and grow are:

Maximize enrollment through new marketing plan; expand reciprocal-referral

program through additional community partners; improve family customer

---

Tom and Juanita used their recent customer survey results, combined with one-on-one discussions with their most loyal families, to determine their key strengths and weaknesses. They used their competitive analysis results and what they've learned about their market over the past few months to identify the greatest opportunities and threats.

Sections 2 through 5: Metrics, Market, Message, and Media

Sections 2 through 5 of the S-MAP are designed to provide you with clarity about each of the four pillars of marketing—metrics, market, message, and media—by asking key questions about the dynamics of each pillar within the context of your program.

In figure 23-2, you can see the S-MAP questions for the Metrics section and how Tom and Juanita answered those questions for ABC Learning Center. Use their example as a model to complete section 2 of your program's Strategic Marketing Action Plan.

Figure 23-2: Metrics Section for ABC Learning Center

Section 2: Metrics

1. What are the measurable goals and objectives you would like to achieve with this plan?

    • *Double our number of inquiries from 10 to 20 per month*

    • *Improve conversion ratio of tours to enrollments by 10 percent*

    • *Improve staff retention by 20 percent*

    • *Improve customer family retention by 20 percent*

2. Do you have the systems in place to provide you with accurate data to measure the goals above?

    Yes. We are using a reliable inquiry-to-enrollment tracking system.

3. If not, what do you need to do to get accurate data?

    n/a

4. Date of last time you completed the nine major metrics defined in part 1 of *The Ultimate Child Care Marketing Guide:*

    July 5, 2011

5. Date of next time metrics will be completed (monthly or quarterly) (add due dates to your calendar):

    August 5, 2011 (monthly metrics), and October 5, 2011 (quarterly metrics)

In figure 23-3, you can see the S-MAP questions for the Market section and how Tom and Juanita answered those questions for ABC Learning Center. Use their example as a model to complete section 3 of your program's Strategic Marketing Action Plan.

Figure 23-3: Market Section for ABC Learning Center

Section 3: Market

1. Describe your typical *current* customer's demographic/geographic and psychographic profiles.

   Our current customer base is approximately 50 percent Caucasian and 50 percent Latino. The average household income is $75K to $125K, parents are 30 to 40 years of age, and they live within a 3-mile radius of our school. They choose our program because it is ethnically diverse and multilingual, as well as a high-quality program with a national accreditation. About 30 percent of our clientele attend through the government assistance program, and 70 percent are private pay.

2. Describe your *desired* target customer's demographic/geographic and psychographic profiles. This may be the same profile as your current customer, or you may wish your customers were more affluent, from a broader geographic area, and so forth.

   We feel our current target customer is a good fit with what we offer, and we don't want to shift our focus to a new market segment. We just need to find more of our target prospects and convert them to customers.

3. What type of customer do you currently attract compared to your competitors?

   We're not completely certain of this, but we believe we attract a higher proportion of Latinos than many of our competitors.

4. What are your current competitive advantages?

We are the only program in the area that offers a fully bilingual curriculum and program. All of our lead teachers are bilingual in both English and Spanish. We are also the only program in the area accredited by NAEYC.

5. What are parents in your market currently seeking in child care that is *not* currently being offered?

Not sure. We will do more market research and focus groups with parents to discover more.

6. What is your unique niche in the marketplace—the things that make your program stand apart from all the other early childhood programs in town?

We are the only program in the area that offers a fully bilingual curriculum and program. All of our lead teachers are bilingual in both English and Spanish. We are also the only program in the area accredited by NAEYC.

7. What are you doing to strengthen your loyalty fence to improve customer retention and average length of enrollment?

New customer satisfaction and communication plan includes more communication every day at pickup time, a monthly newsletter, weekly e-mail updates, and more frequent parent-teacher and parent-director conferences.

8. What percentage of new enrollments is directly due to your referral-rewards program? How are you going to grow this percentage?

We do not currently have a formal referral-rewards program in place. We are planning to launch this within the next three months.

9. Do you have a regular system in place for gathering customer testimonials? If not, add this to your goals and objectives.

   Yes. Our system includes asking parents who tell us something positive to provide a testimonial, as well as holding an annual testimonial contest to gather written and video testimonials for use on our website and on all marketing materials. We are also in the process of framing our best testimonials and hanging them in our hallways and restroom.

In figure 23-4, you can see the S-MAP questions for the Message section and how Tom and Juanita answered those questions for ABC Learning Center. Use their example as a model to complete section 4 of your program's Strategic Marketing Action Plan.

Figure 23-4: Message Section for ABC Learning Center
Section 4: Message

1. What is your unique value statement?

   We are the only program in the area that offers a fully bilingual curriculum and program. All of our lead teachers are bilingual in both English and Spanish. We are also the only program in the area accredited by NAEYC.

2. What are your competitors' unique value statements?

   One of our competitors is a Montessori school. The other key competitor does not appear to have (or is not communicating) a clear UVS.

3. What are the unique benefits you offer to your desired target market?

   - *fully bilingual curriculum and program*

   - *NAEYC accreditation*

   - *flexible scheduling*

   - *monthly parents' night out free of charge*

4. What is your satisfaction guarantee or promise?

   100% Smiles Guarantee: We guarantee you and your child will be 100%

   happy with our school. If not, we will provide you with a full refund of one

   week of tuition, no questions asked.

5. What offers have been the most successful for you in the past?

   We did not use special enrollment offers in the past, other than occasional

   free registration offers. These did not generate much excitement.

6. What new offers would you like to test? (Make sure to include a deadline.)

   One Week Free Plus Free Registration (Up to $300 Value) When You Enroll by

   (specify date)

7. Do all your marketing materials include at least one testimonial? If not, add this to your task list.

   Yes

In figure 23-5, you can see the S-MAP questions for the Media section and how Tom and Juanita answered those questions for ABC Learning Center. Use their example as a model to complete section 5 of your program's Strategic Marketing Action Plan.

Figure 23-5: Media Section for ABC Learning Center

Section 5: Media

1. What media have you used in the past to promote or advertise your program?

   Community events, sporadic press releases, and our website. Mostly we
   relied on word of mouth.

2. Of these, what medium has provided the highest ROI for you?

   We don't know, because at that time we were not tracking ROI.

3. What local media choices are the most targeted to young families in your area?

   Direct mail is the most targeted choice because there is little waste—we
   know we are reaching families with young children in our target area. We
   also found a "Mom with Tots" group that is highly targeted for us, and we
   plan to advertise in their newsletter and place a banner ad on their website.

4. What media are your competitors using?

   Our Montessori competitor uses some newspaper ads and exhibits at most
   local events.

5. What media choices would you like to test?

   We have a large menu of media choices to test over the next quarter. (See
   budget below for detail.)

6. What methods or codes are you going to use to track your results?

We are using unique phone numbers for each media type, as well as unique

landing pages on our website to track the response levels.

7. What is your marketing budget by media type? (Define the time period—quarterly or annual, for example.)

Our quarterly budget is as follows:

Marketing Element	BUDGET
Website and online marketing	$1,350
Community events / publicity	200
Referral-rewards program	800
Direct mail	1,200
Local newspaper ads	250
Moms of Tots club newsletter ads	75
New signage	225
Flyers and brochures	500
TOTAL	**$4,600**

Sections 6 and 7: Your Goals and Tasks

Section 6 of the S-MAP asks you to think about and revise your goals, based on the answers you provided in sections 2 through 5. In figure 23-6, you can see the S-MAP questions for the Goals section and how Tom and Juanita answered those questions for ABC Learning Center. Use their example as a model to complete section 6 of your program's Strategic Marketing Action Plan.

Figure 23-6: Goals Section for ABC Learning Center

Section 6: Revisit and Edit Your Goals

---

1. What additional goals or objectives have you identified? Which do you
   need to accomplish to improve the financial health of your business?

   None. These remain our top four goals:

   • *Double our number of inquiries from 10 to 20 per month*

   • *Improve conversion ratio of tours to enrollments by 10 percent*

   • *Improve staff retention by 20 percent*

   • *Improve customer family retention by 20 percent*

Section 7 of the S-MAP asks you to come up with three to five goals of the
highest priority; that is those goals you believe will get the results you want and
need for your program. In section 7, describe each goal and lay out detailed
action steps for each one, including timeline, task owner, how you will measure
and document the task, and the budget or other resources required to accomplish the task.

In figure 23-7, you can see how the Task Detail section is laid out and how
Tom and Juanita completed it for ABC Learning Center. Use their example as a
model to complete section 7 of your program's Strategic Marketing Action Plan.

Figure 23-7: Action Steps and Timeline for ABC Learning Center

Section 7: Action Steps and Timeline

---

1. Describe each goal and lay out the detailed action steps for it, including the
   timeline, task owner, how you plan to measure and document the task, and
   the budget or other resources required to accomplish the task.

GOAL #1: Double the volume of inquiries from 10 to 20 per month

Task/Action Step	Timeline/ Due Date	Task Owner	Measurement/ Documentation	Budget/ Resources
Revamp website, new videos on website	Aug. 15	Tom	None needed	$1,100
Higher rank (Top 3) on Google for top keywords	Aug. 20	Tom	Tom to audit Google results	$250 to SEO guy
Monthly press releases	Ongoing	Juanita	Juanita to report	—
Direct mail campaign	July 25	Tom	Phone number tracking reports	$1,200

GOAL #2: Improve conversion ratio of tours to enrollments by 10 percent

Task/Action Step	Timeline/ Due Date	Task Owner	Measurement/ Documentation	Budget/ Resources
Add testimonials to prospect packet and walls of center	Aug. 1	Asst Dir.	None needed	$200
Provide coffee, water, juice boxes, and snacks for visitors	Aug. 1	Asst Dir.	None needed	$200
Do a better job of communicating unique differences during tour	July 25	Juanita	None needed	None
Role-play asking for the enrollment—give offer and deadline	July 25	Juanita and team	None needed	None

GOAL #3: Improve staff retention by 20 percent

Task/Action Step	Timeline/ Due Date	Task Owner	Measurement/ Documentation	Budget/ Resources
Team-building activities	Sept. 1	Asst. Dir.	Employee surveys	None
Staff appreciation systems	Sept. 1	Asst. Dir.	Employee surveys	None
Consistent performance reviews	Sept. 15	Juanita	Performance review plan	None
Plan for raises and bonuses	Oct. 1	Juanita	Compensation plan	TBD

GOAL #4: Improve customer family retention by 20 percent

Task/Action Step	Timeline/ Due Date	Task Owner	Measurement/ Documentation	Budget/ Resources
New parent communication system—every day at pickup time	Sept. 1	Juanita	New system in orange binder	Employee training session on Aug. 30
Monthly newsletter	Sept. 1	Asst. Dir.	None needed	$200/ month
Weekly e-mail updates with photos	Sept. 15	Tom	None needed	None
More frequent parent-teacher and parent-director conferences	Oct. 1	Juanita	Conference records	None

Based on the examples we've just reviewed for ABC Learning Center, take the time now to complete your S-MAP. Then track the action steps based on their due dates and to whom they are assigned. If you take the time to get this exercise started now, while your mind is fresh and brimming with ideas, your program will benefit much more than if you wait.

24

Create Systems for Ongoing Success

We've just learned about how to more effectively use a plan to help you succeed in your marketing and enrollment-building efforts. Now let's talk about another important success tool: systems. There are numerous benefits to creating systems in your business; let's look in depth into the what, why, and how of system creation for early childhood businesses.

What Is a System, Anyway?

A *system* can be defined as a set of business procedures that, when consistently used, provide the same desired result each time, regardless of variables such as who uses the system, when they use it, or why they use it. Systems allow you to delegate procedures effectively without worrying about the procedure breaking down. Of course, sometimes systems do break down—and when they do, it's important to document why the breakdown occurred, how it could have been prevented, and what changes should be made so it doesn't happen again.

Compared to many other small businesses, early childhood programs have a great deal of paperwork to manage, due to state licensing requirements, accreditation requirements, and ongoing training paperwork for each employee. Thus, early childhood businesses can benefit even more than most other businesses by putting systems into place to help deal with the demands of administrative tasks—paperwork, timelines, due dates, and regulatory requirements.

When you use systems to help manage the daily operations of your program, your day-to-day experience and that of your employees becomes much easier. That's why many successful child care businesses use child care management software: the software automates tasks (or eliminates certain manual tasks completely) and systemizes the business in many areas of its operations, such as invoicing, payment collection, payroll, parent tax forms, parent communication, safety procedures, and the like.

The mind-set of an owner or director who utilizes systems is that of one who embraces the idea of automating mundane tasks, optimizing productivity and efficiency, working on the business rather than in the business, and spending more time promoting a vision rather than managing nuts and bolts. If this sounds like you, or someone you want to become, you need to develop and implement systems.

Why Use Systems?

The benefits of using systems are many. First, systems save time. They clearly identify the written procedures that allow you and your employees to do your best work, the same time every time. Such written procedures can also be thought of as work instructions—that is, steps to follow for a certain procedure. These instructions should be detailed enough and clear enough that a new employee would be able to follow them (assuming she was properly skilled for the task).

For example, in the past you might have lacked a system for effectively following up with a prospect after the tour. Because you or your director dealt with each follow-up task individually, the follow-up activities took more time than if they were grouped together as a whole (for example, mailing cards or letters as a group versus individually, or sending a blast e-mail to a group of prospects versus sending individual e-mails). When you identify the steps that should be taken each time to follow up with prospects, your system will result in less wasted time and effort, and fewer mistakes.

This brings me to the second biggest benefit: systems save money. The cost of figuring out how to do a procedure, or doing it incorrectly and making mistakes, is very high to your organization. If you have a well-documented system that everyone, including new employees, is trained on, you'll save countless dollars for your program over the long run.

A third benefit of systems is that they build morale. Systems will save you and your team the headaches and exhaustion that come with repeatedly having to fight fires as you do your work. Your employees can take off their firefighter hats and focus on what they were trained to do: teach young children.

Finally, systems add value. Having reliable systems in your business will add value to the parents and families you serve, because your program will be better run, employees' morale will be higher, and you will be able to focus on higher level tasks like growing the business, expanding to new locations, or further improving customer satisfaction. Furthermore, having systems will enable you to sell your business more easily when it's time to move on or retire. If you are a director, you should communicate this value-added benefit to your owner and ask for resources and assistance to systemize the business. If you are an owner, systems will keep your business running without you and make your program less reliant on you, allowing you to pursue new wealth opportunities or reduce your workload.

How to Create Systems

Systems don't have to be complicated to work well—in fact, the simpler the system, the better it tends to work and to stick. Simply write down all the steps you and your staff take to accomplish a specific task or procedure: break down each activity into its key "how-to" steps to create and then document written procedures and instructions. This is the perfect time to examine and analyze the process or procedure to look for ways to improve it. Ask your team of teachers and staff to help you. (You can add a visual component to your system document by embedding photos or images into the document text. These could include screen capture images for procedures that use computer software, or photos of the desired actions and outcomes of your safety systems, for example. Using images in addition to text can make the system easier to comprehend and follow for the user.)

To get started, group activities into categories by how often you do them. Work on daily procedures first, then weekly, monthly, quarterly, and annually.

Or prioritize system creation based on the financial impact of the procedures: document your high-dollar activities first, and then take a look at lower-level ones. How you categorize the work is up to you—the key is to get started and keep going until most of your processes have documented systems to support them, with the goal of identifying and eliminating wasteful effort and errors. Here's a brainstorming exercise to help you identify and prioritize what systems, once created or improved, would most benefit you, your staff, and your program.

Exercise 23 Identify and Prioritize the Need for Systems in Your Business

Answer the following questions using the space provided.

1. According to your program's managers and owners, what are the top three areas of the business that are the most dysfunctional?

    a. _____

    b. _____

    c. _____

2. According to your teachers and child care staff, what are the top three areas of the business that are the most dysfunctional?

    a. _____

    b. _____

    c. _____

3. According to parent customers, what are the top three areas of the business that are the most dysfunctional?

    a. _____

    b. _____

    c. _____

4. Are there any areas listed as dysfunctional by all three groups? Write those here.

a. _____

b. _____

c. _____

5. Now prioritize the areas identified by all three groups by determining which area, if fixed, would have the most positive impact on your program. Communicate these results to staff and, if appropriate, to all parents or to the parent board.

Priority 1: _____

Priority 2: _____

Priority 3: _____

Keep all systems for a related category together in color-coded binders for easy access. For example, keep your enrollment funnel system in a green binder and your parent communication system in a yellow binder. In addition, you could make a video of yourself or a staff member that walks employees through a system; keep the system videos together in a set of DVDs.

 For a long time, Tom and Juanita had known they needed to implement more systems in their program so things would run more smoothly—both in terms of daily operations and their marketing and enrollment processes. They identified one day in the middle of July when they would close the center to hold an in-service day for all the teachers—a day of teamwork and activities designed to improve the way things were run. They started the day with an open brainstorming session, where teachers were asked to help identify and prioritize all the broken processes in the center—those that were counterproductive, disruptive to children or parents, time-wasters, money-wasters—in short, anything that could be considered dysfunctional.

Rather than fostering a gripe session, however, Tom and Juanita were able to keep staff focused on positive aspects of change and the rewards teachers would earn by helping create and implement new or revamped systems in the school. It took about four months to get the top five systems created, implemented, and working smoothly, but by November, the center was running much more smoothly. Parents took notice, and retention rates of both staff and families improved.

It may seem daunting, not to mention a lot of work, to create viable systems in your business. But remember the rewards—systems can save time and large sums of money, improve staff morale and retention of families in your program, and even allow you as the owner or director to get away from the business more often. Put simply, systems add value to your organization.

Final Thoughts

I hope you've learned a ton of strategies, tactics, and tips from this book. You may be experiencing the "my head is about to explode" sensation that sometimes hits me when I learn a large volume of new information. If that is the case, don't worry. By following and using the exercises in this book and using your Strategic Marketing Action Plan, you will be well on the way to taking baby steps (followed by larger breakthroughs) toward improving the effectiveness of your marketing and growing your early childhood program—not just now, but for the rest of your career. I also recommend putting this book down for a month or two, then picking it back up again and rereading it to refresh the information in your mind and remind you of actions you wanted to take. Plus, you will gain some new insights the second time around.

A highly successful client of mine once told me she put my ideas into action slowly but consistently—she referred to it as "eating the elephant one bite at a time." As you learn, grow, and take action, you will continue to improve your results by always measuring and looking for ways to optimize further. Embrace these ideas and implement what you've learned in this book to grow your enrollment and become an entrepreneurial child care leader who's a marketing champion! Remember, if you use your *metrics* to deliver the right *message* to the right *market* using the right *media,* you will become fully enrolled and stay that way over the long term.

I look forward to hearing about your successful journey!

Appendix A: Tour Checklist

Use a checklist to give a successful tour of your program every time.

Printed Materials

☐ Are our promotional and marketing materials stocked and ready?

☐ Is all the information in our promotional and marketing materials current?

☐ Do we have handouts of testimonials or rave reviews ready to share?

☐ Have all of our printed materials been proofread by a third party for spelling and grammar errors?

☐ Are our key marketing message and our unique value statement clearly worded in our tour handouts?

Tour Personnel

☐ Is our program director on hand to provide the tour?

☐ Are all other personnel conducting the tour fully trained and well versed in the program's operations and policies?

☐ Are breath mints available for tour personnel?

Facility Presentation

☐ Is the program facility clean and fresh smelling?

☐ Are the teachers and other staff ready to greet guests warmly as we enter each classroom?

☐ Are materials posted on bulletin boards current?

☐ Are curriculum materials readily available to share with the tour guests?

Communication

☐ Are touring personnel ready to introduce themselves to the touring guests?

☐ If children are present, are the touring personnel ready to engage frequently and sincerely with them?

☐ Are the touring personnel prepared to communicate with the touring guests in a clear and professional manner?

☐ Are the touring personnel prepared to clearly communicate the unique benefits of our program?

☐ Are the touring personnel prepared to conduct a pretour questionnaire with the parents?

☐ Are the touring personnel capable of using information discovered through the pretour questionnaire to enhance the tour?

Appendix B: Sample Parent Survey

As part of our effort to continually improve, we are seeking your input and feedback on your family's experience with ABC Learning Center. Please take a few minutes to complete the following survey. Your responses may be anonymous if you wish. Thank you very much!

1. Please rate the following aspects of your overall experience at ABC. (Please circle one.)

	Poor	Average			Excellent
a. Value for the price paid	1	2	3	4	5
b. Quality of teachers/staff	1	2	3	4	5
c. Curriculum (appropriateness, effectiveness)	1	2	3	4	5
d. Responsiveness of staff to my concerns	1	2	3	4	5
e. Regular communication about your child's progress and daily activities	1	2	3	4	5
f. Cleanliness	1	2	3	4	5
g. Safety and security	1	2	3	4	5
h. Quality of meals and snacks	1	2	3	4	5
i. Other: _____	1	2	3	4	5

2. What one thing do you value most about ABC? _____

_____

_____

3. What one thing would you most like to see improved at ABC? _____

_____

_____

4. We are considering adding a _____ service that would enable

   you to _____. Which of the following best describes

   your reaction to such a service at ABC? (Please check one.)

   ☐ I would love this type of service and would use it often at ABC.

   ☐ Sounds interesting, but I have some concerns, which are:

   _____

   _____

   ☐ I am not interested in such a service.

5. Do you have any other comments or feedback about how we're doing or
   how we can improve? _____

   _____

   _____

6. What are the ages of your children who are enrolled at ABC?

   _____

   _____

7. OPTIONAL: Please provide your name: _____

   _____

Appendix C:
Strategic Marketing Action Plan (S-MAP)

Name of Program/Business: _____

Date/Version: _____

Section 1: SWOT Analysis

S: According to the voices of my customers, the key strengths of my program are:

_____

_____

_____

_____

W: According to the voices of my customers, the key weaknesses of my program are:

_____

_____

_____

_____

O: The key opportunities for my business to prosper and grow are:

_____

_____

_____

_____

T: The key threats to the future of my business are:

_____

_____

_____

_____

Section 2: Metrics

1. What are the measurable goals and objectives you would like to achieve with this plan?

   _____

   _____

   _____

   _____

2. Do you have the systems in place to provide you with accurate data to measure the goals above?

   _____

   _____

   _____

   _____

   _____

3. If not, what do you need to do to get accurate data?

_____

_____

_____

_____

4. Date of last time you completed the full metrics set in part 1 of *The Ultimate Child Care Marketing Guide*: _____

5. Date of next time metrics will be completed (monthly or quarterly) (add due dates to your calendar): _____

Section 3: Market

1. Describe your *current* average target customer's demographic/geographic and psychographic profiles.

_____

_____

_____

_____

2. Describe your *desired* average target customer's demographic/geographic and psychographic profiles. This may be the same profile as your current customer, or you may wish your customers were more affluent, from a broader geographic area, and so forth.

_____

_____

_____

_____

_____

3. What type of customer do you currently attract compared to your competitors?

_____

_____

_____

_____

4. What are your current competitive advantages?

_____

_____

_____

_____

5. What are parents in your market currently seeking in child care that is *not* currently being offered?

_____

_____

_____

_____

6. What is your unique niche in the marketplace—the things that make your program stand apart from all the other early childhood programs in town? What are you doing to strengthen your loyalty fence to customer retention and average length of enrollment? What percentage of new enrollments is directly due to your referral-rewards program? How are you going to grow this percentage?

_____

_____

_____

_____

_____

_____

_____

_____

7. Do you have a regular system in place for gathering customer testimonials? If not, add this to your goals and objectives.

_____

_____

_____

_____

Section 4: Message

1. What is your unique value statement?

_____

_____

_____

_____

2. What are your competitors' unique value statements?

_____

_____

_____

_____

3. What are the unique benefits you offer to your desired target market?

_____

_____

_____

_____

4. What is your satisfaction guarantee or promise?

_____

_____

_____

_____

5. What offers have been the most successful for you in the past?

_____

_____

_____

_____

6. What new offers would you like to test? (Make sure to include a deadline.)

_____

_____

_____

_____

7. Do all your marketing materials include at least one testimonial? If not, add this to your task list. _____

_____

Section 5: Media

1. What media have you used in the past to promote or advertise your
    program?

    _____

    _____

    _____

    _____

2. Of these, what medium has provided the highest ROI for you?

    _____

    _____

    _____

    _____

3. What local media choices are the most targeted to young families in your
    area?

    _____

    _____

    _____

    _____

4. What media are your competitors using?

    _____

    _____

    _____

    _____

    _____

5. What media choices would you like to test?

_____

_____

_____

_____

6. What methods or codes are you going to use to track your results?

_____

_____

_____

_____

7. What is your marketing budget by media type? (Define the period—quarterly or annually, for example.)

_____

_____

_____

_____

Section 6: Revisit and Edit Your Goals

1. What additional goals or objectives have you identified? Which do you need to accomplish to improve the financial health of your business?

_____

_____

_____

_____

2. Based on your responses in Sections 1–5 above, what are the **top 5 action steps** you should take right now to accomplish the goals and objectives you stated in Section 2? (enter into table in next section)

_____

_____

_____

_____

Section 7: Action Steps and Timeline

1. Describe each goal, and lay out the detailed action steps for it, including the timeline, task owner, how you plan to measure and document the task, and the budget or other resources required to accomplish the task.

GOAL #1: _____

_____

Task / Action Step	Timeline / Due Date	Task Owner	Measurement / Documentation	Budget / Resources

GOAL #2: _____

_____

Task / Action Step	Timeline / Due Date	Task Owner	Measurement / Documentation	Budget / Resources

GOAL #3: _____

_____

Task / Action Step	Timeline / Due Date	Task Owner	Measurement / Documentation	Budget / Resources

GOAL #4: _____

_____

Task / Action Step	Timeline / Due Date	Task Owner	Measurement / Documentation	Budget / Resources

GOAL #5: _____

_____

Task / Action Step	Timeline / Due Date	Task Owner	Measurement / Documentation	Budget / Resources

Glossary

advertising: The act or practice of calling public attention to your program, especially by paid announcements in media, such as newspapers, magazines, radio, television, and billboards.

article marketing: The practice of writing articles and providing them to online or offline media to promote your ideas, program, and status as an expert authority.

autoresponder: A simple computer program that automatically sends out marketing and relationship-building e-mail messages on a predetermined schedule.

banner ads: An online advertisement containing a link to your website. These ads are typically displayed on-screen in a rectangle or square.

benefit: A feature communicated to your prospective customers as an advantage offered by your program.

best neighborhood strategy: A strategy for identifying where your best customers and prospects live so you can aggressively market to them.

branding (or **brand image**): The practice of promoting the name of your program and the values you desire consumers to associate with it.

broadcast e-mail (or **e-mail blast**): An e-mail containing newsworthy information that you can send to all your prospects or enrolled families at once.

CCR&R: A child care resource and referral agency. Your local CCR&R is a branch of the National Association of Child Care Resource and Referral Agencies (NACCRRA).

community marketing: Any strategy you use to personally connect with local residents and business partners, such as participation in local events, cross-promotional campaigns with other businesses, and membership in community organizations.

community partners: Local businesses that share your ideal or target customer, such as toy stores, children's clothing stores and consignment shops, family and children's hair salons, pediatricians, pediatric dentists, and real-estate agents who serve young families moving into the area.

conversion ratio of leads to tours: The rate at which people who inquire about your child care program actually come in to your center to take a tour.

conversion ratio of tours to enrollments: The rate at which people who tour your child care center end up enrolling in your program.

cost-per-click: The maximum amount you are willing to spend on a pay-per-click ad.

cost per lead (or **cost per inquiry**): The amount of money you spend, on average, to get one new customer lead.

cost per new customer (or **cost per sale**): The amount of money you spend, on average, to convert one customer lead to one new customer.

curb appeal: The attractiveness of your child care facility and grounds from the outside.

customer retention: The proportion of families who stay enrolled in your center from one period to the next.

customer turnover: The proportion of families who leave your center from one period to the next.

customer value and acquisition metrics: Metrics that illustrate the relationship between the revenue a typical customer family brings to your program compared to the average amount of money you spend to market to and acquire that family as a customer.

demographic profile: The profile of your average customer or client by gender, age, income, presence of children in the home, and other demographic factors.

digital marketing: The practice of marketing through online or electronic media, such as websites, e-mail, smartphones, and SMS messages.

direct mail: Any marketing message you mail directly to your customer's home or workplace in the form of a letter, postcard, greeting card, thank-you note, or gift package.

e-mail management system: Software that enables you to build and manage a database of e-mail contacts and send broadcast e-mails to those contacts.

enrollment funnel: The process you undertake to market and promote your center to generate leads and convert them into enrollments.

enrollment funnel metrics: Metrics that measure the results of each step in your marketing process to determine each step's effectiveness in converting leads to enrollments.

feature: A characteristic of your program, such as extended hours or nutritious meals.

geographic profile: The profile of your average customer or client in terms of where they live or work.

gross revenue (or **tuition revenue** or **gross sales**): The amount of money your program earns in sales from all revenue sources.

inbound links: Links to your business's web page(s) that are placed on other websites. These can be links you pay for—such as on banner ads—or free links provided by organizations you are a member of, business partners, free online directories, and so on.

keywords: The most common words and phrases your prospects use to find your service or product when searching the Internet.

know-like-trust principle: A rule of thumb that people do business with people they know, like, and trust.

lead (or **prospect** or **inquiry**): A prospective customer who contacts you for more information about your program.

lead generation advertising (or **two-step marketing**): A form of advertising that offers prospects a free gift or special deal to get them to show interest in what your ad is offering.

lifetime customer value (LCV) (or **total customer value**): The monetary value a typical customer brings to your business, in gross revenue or in net revenue, over the time he does business with you.

loyalty fence: The strength of your bond with your customer families, which prevents your customers from doing business with one of your competitors. When your customers are highly loyal to doing business with you, you have a strong loyalty fence.

market: The area where your business is located, as well as the people who live or work there.

marketing: All of the activities involved in getting and keeping customers.

marketing copy: Written promotional material in ads, flyers, brochures, and web pages.

marketing plan: The plan for an advertising or promotional campaign, including decisions about which media you will use, when they will be used, how much you will spend, and what you hope to accomplish with each medium.

marketing return on investment (ROI) metrics: Data about every action you take to advertise, promote, and market your program in terms of revenue generated by those efforts compared to their cost.

market match: Prospective customers who are a good fit for your program.

market segment (or **niche**): A group of people within your market who have something in common, such as customers who are parents of toddlers.

media: The methods you use to promote and advertise your program, such as through newspapers, magazines, the radio, television, websites, direct mail, e-mail, social media, and so on.

message: The words, images, and ideas in your marketing materials and efforts.

metrics: The numbers and data you track in your business that indicate how your business and marketing efforts are performing. This book covers nine key business metrics, broken into four categories: customer value and acquisition metrics, enrollment funnel metrics, marketing return on investment metrics, and retention rate metrics.

net revenue (or **net operating income**): The amount of money that remains in your business after you take into account all of the operating costs and expenses required to deliver your services over a given period.

online directories: Websites on which you can list your child care business.

operating margin: A ratio used to measure your program's pricing strategy and operating efficiency.

opt-in forms: The space on a website where a potential customer provides contact information for more information about your program.

paid traffic source: A website tracking program that measures which online sources generate the highest number of targeted leads for your program.

pay-per-click (PPC) advertising: A form of Internet advertising for which you pay a fee each time a potential customer clicks on your ad. Google is one of the most popular pay-per-click providers.

problem-agitate-solve copywriting technique: A formula for writing marketing copy: present a problem, agitate the problem, and then solve the problem.

publicity: Public attention through any media outlet, such as newspapers, magazines, and radio and television stations.

raw number of leads: The total number of prospective families who inquire about your child care program during a given period.

referral-rewards program: An incentive program that rewards current customers for referring others to your business.

retention rate metrics: Metrics that provide you with a picture of how well and how long you hold on to two key resources in your program: customers and staff.

search engine optimization (SEO): The practice of optimizing your website to capture your top search phrases or keywords.

sequential mail campaigns: A series of mailings that are sent to the same list of people each time to boost responses. Campaigns often involve a sequence of three mailings sent a week apart.

social media: Websites that allow visitors to interact with one another, identify common interests, share photos, and so on.

social proof: A psychological phenomenon where people assume the actions of others reflect the correct behavior for a given situation. A very positive testimonial or referral that gives a credible demonstration of the benefits of a product or service is a form of social proof.

staff retention: The proportion of staff members who continue working for your program from one period to the next.

staff turnover: The proportion of staff members who leave your program from one period to the next.

supply and demand: The amount of a certain product or service available in a given market (supply) compared to the amount of consumers who need or desire that product or service (demand). A product's or service's supply and demand can be used to determine price levels; for example, when supply is low and demand is high, the price for a product or service typically increases.

sweet spot: A market segment that is more responsive or profitable than the general market.

SWOT analysis: An analysis of your program's current strengths, weaknesses, opportunities, and threats.

system: A set of business procedures that, when consistently used, provide the same desired result each time, regardless of variables such as who uses the system, when they use it, or why they use it.

tagline (or **slogan**): A phrase used in conjunction with your company logo to describe your brand image.

target market: The demographic and psychographic description of a consumer group designated as the current or prospective users of your product or service.

targeted traffic: The total number of leads or prospects in your target market that visit your website or inquire about your product or service.

testimonial: An endorsement from a current customer.

three-dimensional (3-D) mail (or **lumpy mail**): A direct marketing mailing that is bulkier than a standard mailing because it holds a three-dimensional object or because it is sent in unusual packaging.

traffic: The number of visitors to your website in a given period or the number of prospective customers who visit your business in a given period.

unique identifier: A unique code or phrase that allows you to track the number of leads a specific marketing activity generates.

unique value statement (UVS) (or **unique selling proposition**): A statement that answers the question, "Why should a customer choose your program instead of any other child care business in town?"

About the Author

Kris Murray is president and founder of Child Care Marketing Solutions. She has over twenty-three years of experience in marketing and business and has focused exclusively on the early childhood industry since 2009. As a business coach and marketing consultant for the early childhood industry, Kris's mission is to help child care owners and directors become more successful and profitable through proven cutting-edge marketing techniques and a unique approach to running a child care business.

Kris has helped hundreds of child care leaders around the world dramatically grow their enrollment, get a better return from their marketing dollars, create systems in their business to save time and improve customer service, and have more fun in their business.

Kris is a professional speaker and has contributed to various early childhood conferences on the topics of enrollment building, marketing, management, and leadership. She is happily married with two children and lives in northeastern Ohio. For more information, please visit Kris's website at www.childcare-marketing.com.